T0305752

Econometric Models for Industrial Organization

World Scientific Lecture Notes in Economics

ISSN: 2382-6118

Series Editor: Ariel Dinar *(University of California, Riverside, USA)*

World Scientific Lecture Notes in Economics – Vol. 3

Econometric Models for Industrial Organization

Matthew Shum

Caltech

World Scientific

NEW JERSEY · LONDON · SINGAPORE · BEIJING · SHANGHAI · HONG KONG · TAIPEI · CHENNAI · TOKYO

Published by

World Scientific Publishing Co. Pte. Ltd.

5 Toh Tuck Link, Singapore 596224

USA office: 27 Warren Street, Suite 401-402, Hackensack, NJ 07601

UK office: 57 Shelton Street, Covent Garden, London WC2H 9HE

Library of Congress Cataloging-in-Publication Data
Names: Shum, Matthew, author.
Title: Econometric models for industrial organization / Matthew Shum (Caltech).
Description: New Jersey : World Scientific, [2016] | Series: World scientific lecture notes in
    economics ; volume 3 | Includes bibliographical references.
Identifiers: LCCN 2016030091 | ISBN 9789813109650 (hc : alk. paper)
Subjects: LCSH: Industrial organization (Economic theory)--Econometric models.
Classification: LCC HD2326 .S5635 2016 | DDC 338.601/5195--dc23
LC record available at https://lccn.loc.gov/2016030091

British Library Cataloguing-in-Publication Data
A catalogue record for this book is available from the British Library.

Desk Editors: Herbert Moses/Alisha Nguyen

Typeset by Stallion Press
Email: enquiries@stallionpress.com

Printed in Singapore

Preface

These lecture notes were conceived and refined over a period of over 10 years, as teaching materials for a one-term course in empirical industrial organization for doctoral or masters students in economics. Students should be familiar with intermediate probability and statistics, although I have attempted to make the lecture notes as self-contained as possible. As lecture notes, these chapters have a breezy tone and style which I use in my classroom lectures. Furthermore, I find it effective to teach otherwise technically difficult topics via close reading of representative papers. Like many of the "newer" fields in economics, empirical industrial organization is better encapsulated as a canon of papers than a set of tools or models; hence commentaries as I have provided for papers in this canon may be the most useful and pedagogically efficient way to absorb the substance.

In any case, as lecture notes the material here is not exhaustive in any way; on the contrary, they are breezy, eclectic, and idiosyncratic — but ultimately sincere and well-intentioned. Any reader who makes it through these notes should find herself upon a secure base from which she can freely pivot towards unexplored terrains. As supplemental materials, I can recommend a good upper-level econometrics text, the *Handbooks of Industrial Organization*, and of course the research papers. Good luck and have fun!

Author's Biography

 Matthew Shum received his Ph.D. in Economics from Stanford University in 1998. He has taught at the University of Toronto, Johns Hopkins University, and the California Institute of Technology. He currently resides in Arcadia, California with his wife and four children.

Acronyms

BBL — Bajari–Benkard–Levin
BLP — Berry–Levinsohn–Pakes
CDF — Cumulative Distribution Function
CS — Confidence Sets
DO — Dynamic Optimization
EDF — Empirical Distribution Function
FOC — First-Order Condition
FWER — Family-wise Error Rate
GHK — Geweke–Hajivassiliou–Keane
GMM — Generalized Method of Moments
HM — Hotz–Miller
LL fxn — Lorentz–Lorenz function
OLS — Ordinary Least Squares

Contents

Chapter 1

Demand Estimation for Differentiated-product Markets

1.1 Why Demand Analysis/Estimation?

There is a huge literature in recent empirical industrial organization (IO) which focuses on estimation of demand models. Why?

Demand estimation seems mundane. Indeed, most IO theory is concerned about supply-side (firm-side). However, important determinants of firm behavior are **costs**, which are usually unobserved.

For instance, consider a fundamental question in empirical IO: how much market power do firms have? Market power is measured by markup: $\frac{p-mc}{p}$. **Problem:** mc not observed! For example, you observe high prices in an industry. Is this due to market power, or due to high costs? We cannot answer this question directly, because we do not observe costs.

The "new empirical industrial organization" (NEIO; a moniker coined by Bresnahan, 1989) is motivated by this data problem. NEIO takes an *indirect approach*, whereby we obtain estimate of firms' markups by estimating firms' demand functions.

Intuition is most easily seen in monopoly, for example:

- $\max_{p} pq(p) - C(q(p))$, where $q(p)$ is the demand curve.
- FOC: $q(p) + pq'(p) = C'(q(p))q'(p)$.

1

- At optimal price p^*, **Inverse Elasticity Property** holds:

$$(p^* - MC(q(p^*))) = -\frac{q(p^*)}{q'(p^*)}$$

or

$$\frac{p^* - mc\,(q(p^*))}{p^*} = -\frac{1}{\epsilon(p^*)},$$

where $\epsilon(p^*)$ is $q'(p^*)\dfrac{p^*}{q(p^*)}$, the price elasticity of demand.

- Hence, if we can estimate $\epsilon(p^*)$, we can infer what the markup $\frac{p^*-mc(q(p^*))}{p^*}$ is, even when we don't observe the marginal cost $mc\,(q(p^*))$.
- Similar exercise holds for oligopoly case (as we will show below).
- Caveat: validity of exercise depends crucially on using the right supply-side model (in this case: monopoly without entry possibility).

If costs were observed: markup could be estimated directly, and we could test for validity of monopoly pricing model (i.e., test whether markup $= \frac{-1}{\epsilon}$).

In these notes, we begin by reviewing some standard approaches to demand estimation, and motivate why recent literature in empirical IO has developed new methodologies.

1.2   Review: Demand Estimation

- Linear demand–supply model:

$$\text{Demand: } q_t^d = \gamma_1 p_t + \mathbf{x'_{t1}}\boldsymbol{\beta_1} + u_{t1},$$
$$\text{Supply: } p_t = \gamma_2 q_t^s + \mathbf{x'_{t2}}\boldsymbol{\beta_2} + u_{t2},$$
$$\text{Equilibrium: } q_t^d = q_t^s.$$

- Demand function summarizes consumer preferences; supply function summarizes firms' cost structure.
- Focus on estimating demand function:

$$\text{Demand: } q_t = \gamma_1 p_t + \mathbf{x'_{t1}}\boldsymbol{\beta_1} + u_{t1}.$$

- If u_1 correlated with u_2, then p_t is endogenous in demand function: cannot be estimated using OLS. Important problem.
- Instrumental variable (IV) methods: assume there are instruments Z's so that $E(u_1 \cdot \mathbf{Z}) = 0$.
- Properties of appropriate instrument Z for endogenous variable p:

  1. Uncorrelated with error term in demand equation: $E(u_1 Z) = 0$. **Exclusion** restriction (order condition).
  2. Correlated with endogenous variable: $E(Zp) \neq 0$ (rank condition).

- The x's are exogenous variables which can serve as instruments:

  1. x_{t2} are *cost shifters*; affect production costs. Correlated with p_t but not with u_{t1}: use as instruments in demand function.
  2. x_{t1} are *demand shifters*; affect willingness-to-pay, but not a firm's production costs. Correlated with q_t but not with u_{2t}: use as instruments in supply function.

The demand models used in empirical IO are different in flavor from "traditional" demand specifications. Start by briefly showing traditional approach, then motivating why that approach does not work for many of the markets that we are interested in.

1.2.1 "Traditional" approach to demand estimation

- Consider modeling demand for two goods 1, 2 (Example: food and clothing).
- Data on prices and quantities of these two goods across consumers, across markets, or over time.
- Consumer demand determined by utility maximization problem:

$$\max_{x_1, x_2} U(x_1, x_2) \quad \text{s.t. } p_1 x_2 + p_2 x_2 = M.$$

- This yields demand functions $x_1^*(p_1, p_2, M)$, $x_2^*(p_1, p_2, M)$.
- Equivalently, start out with *indirect utility function*,

$$V(p_1, p_2, M) = U(x_1^*(p_1, p_2, M), x_2^*(p_1, p_2, M)).$$

- Demand functions derived via *Roy's Identity*:

$$x_1^*(p_1, p_2, M) = -\frac{\partial V}{\partial p_1} \bigg/ \frac{\partial V}{\partial M},$$

$$x_2^*(p_1, p_2, M) = -\frac{\partial V}{\partial p_2} \bigg/ \frac{\partial V}{\partial M}.$$

This approach is often more convenient empirically.
- This "standard" approach is not convenient for many markets which we are interested in: automobile, airlines, cereals, toothpaste, etc. These markets are characterized by:

  — Many alternatives: too many parameters to estimate using traditional approach.
  — At individual level, usually only choose one of the available options (discrete choices). Consumer demand function not characterized by FOC of utility maximization problem.

These problems have been addressed by:

  — Modeling demand for a product as demand for the characteristics of that product: **Hedonic** analysis (Rosen, 1974; Bajari and Benkard, 2005).

    This can be difficult in practice when there are many characteristics, and the characteristics are not continuous.
  — Discrete choice: assume each consumer can choose at most *one* of the available alternatives on each purchase occasion. This is the approach taken in the modern empirical IO literature.

1.3   Discrete-choice Approach to Modeling Demand

- Starting point: McFadden's (1978, 1981) *random utility* framework.
- There are N alternatives in market $j = 1, \ldots, N$. In each purchase occasion, each consumer i divides her income y_i on (at most) one of the alternatives, and on an "outside good":

$$\max_{j,z} U_i(x_j, z) \quad \text{s.t. } p_j + p_z z = y_i,$$

where

- x_j are characteristics of brand j, and p_j the price
- z is quantity of outside good, and p_z its price
- outside good $(j = 0)$ denotes the nonpurchase of any alternative (that is, spending entire income on other types of goods).

- Substitute in the budget constraint $(z = \frac{y-p_n}{p_z})$ to derive *conditional indirect utility functions* for each brand:

$$U_{ij}^* = U_i \left(x_j, \frac{y - p_j}{p_z} \right).$$

If outside good is bought:

$$U_{i0}^* = U_i \left(0, \frac{y}{p_z} \right).$$

- Consumer chooses the brand yielding the highest conditional indirect utility:

$$\max_j U_{ij}^*.$$

- U_{ij}^* is specified as sum of two parts. The first part is a function $V_{ij}(\cdots)$ of the observed variables (prices, characteristics, etc.). The second part is a "utility shock," consisting of choice-affecting elements not observed by the econometrician:

$$U_{ij}^* = V_{ij}(p_j, p_z, y_i) + \epsilon_{ij}.$$

The utility shock ϵ_{ij} is observed by agent i, not by econometrician: we call this a **structural error**. From agent's point of view, utility and choice are *deterministic*.

- Given this specification, the probability that consumer i buys brand j is:

$$D_{ij} = \text{Prob} \left\{ \epsilon_{i0}, \dots, \epsilon_{iN} : U_{ij}^* > U_{ij'}^* \text{ for } j' \neq j \right\}.$$

If households are identical, so that $V_{ij} = V_{i'j}$ for i, i', and $\vec{\epsilon} \equiv \{\epsilon_{i0}, \dots, \epsilon_{iN}\}'$ is identically and independently distributed (i.i.d.) across agents i (and there are a very large number of agents), then D_{ij} is also the *aggregate market share*.

- Hence, specific distributional assumptions on $\vec{\epsilon}$ determine the functional form of choice probabilities. Two common distributional assumptions are:

  1. $(\epsilon_{i0}, \dots, \epsilon_{iN})$ distributed multivariate normal: **multinomial probit**. Choice probabilities do not have closed form, but they can be simulated (Keane, 1994; McFadden, 1989). (Cf. GHK simulator, which we describe in a different set of lecture notes.)

     But model becomes awkward when there are large number of choices, because number of parameters in the variance matrix Σ also grows very large.

  2. $(\epsilon_{ij}, \ j = 0, \dots, N)$ i.i.d. type I extreme value across i:

  $$ F(\epsilon) = \exp\left[-\exp\left(-\frac{\epsilon - \eta}{\mu} \right) \right], $$

  with the location parameter $\eta = 0.577$ (Euler's constant), and the scale parameter (usually) $\mu = 1$.

  This leads to multinomial logit (MNL) choice probabilities:

  $$ D_{ij}(\cdots) = \frac{\exp(V_{ij})}{\sum_{j'=1,\dots,N} \exp(V_{ij'})}. $$

  Normalize $V_0 = 0$. (Because $\sum_{j=1}^{N} D_{ij} = 1$ by construction.)

  Convenient, tractable form for choice probabilities, which scales easily when the number of goods increases. For this reason, the MNL model is basis for many demand papers in empirical IO.

Problems with MNL

Despite its tractability, the MNL model has restrictive implications, which are particularly unattractive for its use in a demand setting. Specifically: the odds ratio between any two brands j, j' does not depend on the number of alternatives available

$$ \frac{D_j}{D_{j'}} = \frac{\exp(V_j)}{\exp(V_{j'})}. $$

Example: Red bus (RB)/blue bus (BB) problem:

- Assume that city has two transportation schemes: walk, and RB, with shares 50% and 50%. So odds ratio of walk/RB $= 1$.
- Now consider introduction of third option: train. Independence of irrelevant alternatives (IIA) implies that odds ratio between walk/RB is still 1. Unrealistic: if train substitutes more with bus than walking, then new shares could be walk 45%, RB 30%, train 25%, then odds ratio walk/RB $= 1.5$.
- What if the third option was BB? IIA implies that the odds ratio between walk/red bus would still be 1. Unrealistic: BB is perfect substitute for RB, so that new shares are walk 50%, RB 25%, BB 25%, and odds ratio walk/RB $= 2$!
- So this is especially troubling if you want to use logit model to predict penetration of new products.

Implication: invariant to introduction (or elimination) of some alternatives. **Independence of Irrelevant Alternatives** (IIA).

If D_{ij} interpreted as market share, IIA implies restrictive substitution patterns:

$$\varepsilon_{a,c} = \varepsilon_{b,c}, \quad \text{for all brands } a, b \neq c.$$

If $V_j = \beta_j + \alpha(y - p_j)$, then $\varepsilon_{a,c} = -\alpha p_c D_c$, for all $c \neq a$: Price decrease in brand a attracts proportionate chunk of demand from all other brands. Unrealistic!

Because of this, the MNL model has been "tweaked" in order to eliminate the implications of IIA:

1. Nested logit: assume particular correlation structure among $(\epsilon_{i0}, \ldots, \epsilon_{iN})$. Within-nest brands are "closer substitutes" than across-nest brands. This model is generated by assuming that the utility shocks $\vec{\epsilon}$ follow a "generalized extreme value" distribution, cf. Maddala (1983, Chapter 2). See Goldberg (1995) for an application of this to automobile demand.

   (Diagram of demand structure from Goldberg paper. One shortcoming of this approach is that the researcher must know the "tree structure" of the model).

2. Random coefficients: assume logit model, but for agent i:

$$U_{ij}^* = X_j'\beta_i - \alpha_i p_j + \epsilon_{ij},$$

(coefficients are agent-specific). This allows for valuations of characteristics, and price-sensitivities, to vary across households. But note that, unlike nested logit model, IIA is still present at the individual-level decision-making problem here; the individual-level choice probability is still MNL in form:

$$D_{ij} = \frac{\exp\left(X_j'\beta_i - \alpha_i p_j\right)}{\sum_{j'} \exp\left(X_{j'}'\beta_i - \alpha_i p_{j'}\right)}.$$

But aggregate market share is

$$\int \frac{\exp\left(X_j'\beta_i - \alpha_i p_j\right)}{\sum_{j'} \exp\left(X_{j'}'\beta_i - \alpha_i p_{j'}\right)} \cdot dF(\alpha_i, \beta_i),$$

and differs from individual choice probability. At the aggregate level, IIA property disappears.

We will focus on this model below, because it has been much used in the recent literature.

1.4   Berry (1994) Approach to Estimate Demand in Differentiated Product Markets

Methodology for estimating differentiated-product discrete-choice demand models, using aggregate data.

Data structure: *cross-section* of market shares:

j	$\hat{s}_j$ (%)	p_j (\$)	X_1	X_2
A	25	1.50	Red	Large
B	30	2.00	Blue	Small
C	45	2.50	Green	Large

Total market size: M
J brands

Note: This is different data structure than that considered in previous contexts: here, all variation is across brands (and no variation across time or markets).

Background: Trajtenberg (1989) study of demand for CAT scanners. Disturbing finding: coefficient on price is *positive*, implying that people prefer more expensive machines! Upward-sloping demand curves.

(Tables of results from Trajtenberg paper)

Possible explanation: quality differentials across products not adequately controlled for. In equilibrium of a differentiated product market where each product is valued on the basis of its characteristics, brands with highly-desired characteristics (higher quality) command higher prices. Unobserved quality leads to price endogeneity.

Here, we start out with the simplest setup, with most restrictive assumptions, and later describe more complicated extensions.

Derive market-level share expression from model of discrete-choice at the individual household level (i indexes household, j is brand):

$$U_{ij} = \underbrace{X_j\beta - \alpha p_j + \xi_j}_{\equiv \delta_j} + \epsilon_{ij},$$

where we call δ_j the "mean utility" for brand j (the part of brand j's utility which is common across all households i).

Econometrician observes neither ξ_j or ϵ_{ij}, but household i observes both: these are both "structural errors."

$\xi_1, \ldots, \xi_J$ are interpreted as "unobserved quality." All else equal, consumers are more willing to pay for brands for which ξ_j is high.

Important: ξ_j, as unobserved quality, is correlated with price p_j (and also potentially with characteristics X_j). It is the source of the endogeneity problem in this demand model.

Make logit assumption that $\epsilon_{ij} \sim$ i.i.d. TIEV, across consumers i and brands j.

Define choice indicators:

$$y_{ij} = \begin{cases} 1 & \text{if } i \text{ chooses brand } j \\ 0 & \text{otherwise.} \end{cases}$$

Table 1.1: MNL Estimates for Body CT Scanners (Quadratic Form with Residual Price).

	1976	1977	1978	1979	1980	1981
RPRICE	11.252	0.993	1.020	0.485	0.695	−0.277
	(6.4)	(4.8)	(4.8)	(1.8)	(2.4)	(−2.5)
SPEED	−2.292	2.138	4.624	−8.669	11.347	−7.504
	(−7.3)	(2.8)	(1.0)	(−1.5)	(2.0)	(−0.5)
SPEED^2	0.236	−1.264	−8.283	31.292	−34.838	74.161
	(4.0)	(−3.4)	(−0.6)	(1.9)	(−1.6)	(1.4)
RESOL	69.107	9.113	−34.126	−15.283	−18.129	32.877
	(7.3)	(2.4)	(−6.3)	(−5.0)	(−3.6)	(−3.9)
RESOL^2	−23.360	−2.533	15.096	6.291	7.738	−24.028
	(−7.6)	(−1.5)	(5.8)	(3.8)	(2.7)	(−4.2)
RTIME	−3.931	5.082	2.385	3.288	3.161	−2.591
	(−5.3)	(7.0)	(2.0)	(3.3)	(2.8)	(−2.8)
RTIME^2	1.054	−2.370	−1.511	−1.401	−2.093	5.560
	(4.5)	(−6.7)	(−2.0)	(−2.1)	(−2.2)	(3.9)
$\rho^2 = 1 - [L(\beta^*)/ L(\beta^0)]$	0.29	0.12	0.16	0.16	0.20	0.14
Corr(π^*, π)	0.999	0.877	0.900	0.870	0.722	0.547
	(0.0001)	(0.0001)	(0.0001)	(0.0001)	(0.0024)	(0.082)
Number of scanners	8	15	16	16	15	11
Number of observations	285	324	164	177	193	153

Note: Asymptotic *t*-values are in parentheses.

Given these assumptions (Table 1.1), choice probabilities take MNL form:

$$Pr\left(y_{ij} = 1|\beta, x_{j'}, \xi_{j'}, j' = 1, \ldots, J\right) = \frac{\exp\left(\delta_j\right)}{\sum_{j'=0}^{J} \exp\left(\delta_{j'}\right)}.$$

Aggregate market shares are:

$$s_j = \frac{1}{M}\left[M \cdot Pr\left(y_{ij} = 1|\beta, x_{j'}, \xi_{j'}, j' = 1, \ldots, J\right)\right] = \frac{\exp\left(\delta_j\right)}{\sum_{j'=1}^{J} \exp\left(\delta_{j'}\right)}$$

$$\equiv \tilde{s}_j\left(\delta_0, \delta_1, \ldots, \delta_J\right) \equiv \tilde{s}_j\left(\alpha, \beta, \xi_1, \ldots, \xi_J\right).$$

$\tilde{s}(\cdots)$ is the "predicted share" function, for fixed values of the parameters α and β, and the unobservables $\xi_1, \ldots, \xi_J$.

- Data contains observed shares: denoted by $\hat{s}_j, j = 1, \ldots, J$
  (Share of outside good is just $\hat{s}_0 = 1 - \sum_{j=1}^{J} \hat{s}_j$).
- Model + parameters give you predicted shares: $\tilde{s}_j(\alpha, \beta, \xi_1, \ldots, \xi_J)$, $j = 1, \ldots, J$.
- Principle: Estimate parameters α, β by finding those values which "match" observed shares to predicted shares: find α, β so that $\tilde{s}_j(\alpha, \beta)$ is as close to $\hat{s}_j$ as possible, for $j = 1, \ldots, J$.
- How to do this? Note that you cannot do **nonlinear least squares** (NLS), i.e.,

$$\min_{\alpha, \beta} \sum_{j=1}^{J} (\hat{s}_j - \tilde{s}_j(\alpha, \beta, \xi_1, \ldots, \xi_J))^2. \tag{1.1}$$

This problem doesn't fit into standard NLS framework, because you need to know the ξ's to compute the predicted share, and they are not observed.

Berry (1994) suggests a clever IV-based estimation approach. Assume there exist instruments Z so that $E(\xi Z) = 0$. Sample analog of this moment condition is

$$\frac{1}{J} \sum_{j=1}^{J} \xi_j Z_j = \frac{1}{J} \sum_{j=1}^{J} (\delta_j - X_j \beta + \alpha p_j) Z_j,$$

which converges (as $J \to \infty$) to zero at the true values α_0, β_0. We wish then to estimate (α, β) by minimizing the sample moment conditions.

Problem with estimating: we do not know δ_j! Berry suggests a *two-step approach*.

First step: Inversion

- If we equate $\hat{s}_j$ to $\tilde{s}_j(\delta_0, \delta_1, \ldots, \delta_J)$, for all j, and normalize $\delta_0 = 0$, we get a system of J nonlinear equations in the J

unknowns $\delta_1, \ldots, \delta_J$:

$$\hat{s}_1 = \tilde{s}_J (\delta_1, \ldots, \delta_J)$$

$$\vdots \qquad \vdots$$

$$\hat{s}_J = \tilde{s}_J (\delta_1, \ldots, \delta_J).$$

- You can "invert" this system of equations to solve for $\delta_1, \ldots, \delta_J$ as a function of the observed $\hat{s}_1, \ldots, \hat{s}_J$.
- Note: the outside good is $j = 0$. Since $1 = \sum_{j=0}^{J} \hat{s}_j$ by construction, you normalize $\delta_0 = 0$.
- Output from this step: $\hat{\delta}_j \equiv \delta_j (\hat{s}_1, \ldots, \hat{s}_J)$, $j = 1, \ldots, J$ (J numbers).

Second step: IV estimation

- Going back to definition of δ_j's:

$$\delta_1 = X_1\beta - \alpha p_1 + \xi_1$$

$$\vdots \qquad \vdots$$

$$\delta_J = X_J\beta - \alpha p_J + \xi_J.$$

- Now, using estimated $\hat{\delta}_j$'s, you can calculate sample moment condition:

$$\frac{1}{J} \sum_{j=1}^{J} \left(\hat{\delta}_j - X_j\beta + \alpha p_j \right) Z_j,$$

and solve for α, β which minimizes this expression.
- If δ_j is linear in X, p, and ξ (as here), then linear IV methods are applicable here. For example, in 2SLS, you regress p_j on Z_j in first stage, to obtain fitted prices $\hat{p}(Z_j)$. Then in second stage, you regress δ_j on X_j and $\hat{p}(Z_j)$.

Later, we will consider the substantially more complicated case when the underlying demand model is the random-coefficients logit model, as in Berry, Levinsohn, and Pakes (1995).

What are appropriate instruments (Berry, 1994, p. 249)?

- Usual demand case: cost shifters. But since we have cross-sectional (across brands) data, we require instruments to verify across brands in a market.
- Take the example of automobiles. In traditional approach, one natural cost shifter could be wages in Michigan.
- But here it does not work, because its the same across all car brands (specifically, if you ran 2SLS with wages in Michigan as the IV, first stage regression of price p_j on wage would yield the same predicted price for all brands).
- BLP exploit competition within market to derive instruments. They use IV's like: characteristics of cars of competing manufacturers. Intuition: oligopolistic competition makes firm j set p_j as a function of characteristics of cars produced by firms $i \neq j$ (e.g., GM's price for the Hum-Vee will depend on how closely substitutable a Jeep is with a Hum-Vee). However, characteristics of rival cars should not affect households' valuation of firm j's car.
- In multiproduct context, similar argument for using characteristics of all other cars produced by same manufacturer as IV.
- With panel dataset, where prices and market shares for same products are observed across many markets, could also use prices of product j in other markets as instrument for price of product j in market t (e.g., Nevo, 2001; Hausman, 1996).

One simple case of inversion step:

MNL case: predicted share $\tilde{s}_j\left(\delta_1, \ldots, \delta_J\right) = \frac{\exp(\delta_j)}{1 + \sum_{j'=1}^{J} \exp(\delta_{j'})}$.

The system of equations from matching actual to predicted shares is:

$$\hat{s}_0 = \frac{1}{1 + \sum_{j=1}^{J} \exp(\delta_j)},$$

$$\hat{s}_1 = \frac{\exp(\delta_1)}{1 + \sum_{j=1}^{J} \exp(\delta_j)}$$

$$\vdots \qquad \vdots$$

$$\hat{s}_J = \frac{\exp(\delta_J)}{1 + \sum_{j=1}^{J} \exp(\delta_j)}.$$

Taking logs, we get system of linear equations for δ_j's:

$$\log \hat{s}_1 = \delta_1 - \log\left(\text{denom}\right)$$

$$\vdots \qquad \vdots$$

$$\log \hat{s}_J = \delta_J - \log\left(\text{denom}\right),$$
$$\log \hat{s}_0 = 0 - \log\left(\text{denom}\right),$$

which yield

$$\delta_j = \log \hat{s}_j - \log \hat{s}_0, \quad j = 1, \ldots, J.$$

So in the second step, run IV regression of

$$\left(\log \hat{s}_j - \log \hat{s}_0\right) = X_j\beta - \alpha p_j + \xi_j. \qquad (1.2)$$

Equation (1.2) is called a "logistic regression" by bio-statisticians, who use this logistic transformation to model "grouped" data. So in the simplest MNL, the estimation method can be described as "logistic IV regression."

See Berry's paper for additional examples (nested logit, vertical differentiation).

1.4.1   Measuring market power: Recovering markups

- Next, we show how demand estimates can be used to derive estimates of firms' markups (as in monopoly example from the beginning).
- From our demand estimation, we have estimated the demand function for brand j, which we denote as follows:

$$D^j \left(\underbrace{X_1, \ldots, X_J}_{\equiv \vec{X}}; \underbrace{p_1, \ldots, p_J}_{\equiv \vec{p}}; \underbrace{\xi_1, \ldots, \xi_J}_{\equiv \vec{\xi}} \right).$$

- Specify costs of producing brand j:

$$C^j \left(q_j, w_j, \omega_j \right),$$

where q_j is total production of brand j, w_j are observed cost components associated with brand j (e.g., could be characteristics of brand j), ω_j are unobserved cost components (another structural error).

- Then profits for brand j are:

$$\Pi_j = D^j(\vec{X}, \vec{p}, \vec{\xi})p_j - C^j(D^j(\vec{X}, \vec{p}, \vec{\xi}), w_j, \omega_j).$$

- For multiproduct firm: assume that firm k produces all brands $j \in \mathcal{K}$. Then its profits are:

$$\tilde{\Pi}_k = \sum_{j \in \mathcal{K}} \Pi_j = \sum_{j \in \mathcal{K}} \left[D^j(\vec{X}, \vec{p}, \vec{\xi})p_j - C^j(D^j(\vec{X}, \vec{p}, \vec{\xi}), w_j, \omega_j) \right].$$

Importantly, we assume that there are no (dis-)economies of scope, so that production costs are simply additive across car models, for a multiproduct firm.

- In order to proceed, we need to assume a particular model of oligopolistic competition.

    The most common assumption is *Bertrand (price) competition*. (Note that because firms produce differentiated products, Bertrand solution does not result in marginal cost pricing.)

- Under price competition, equilibrium prices are characterized by J equations (which are the J pricing first-order conditions for the J brands):

$$\frac{\partial \tilde{\Pi}_k}{\partial p_j} = 0, \ \forall j \in \mathcal{K}, \ \forall k$$

$$\Leftrightarrow D^j + \sum_{j' \in \mathcal{K}} \frac{\partial D^{j'}}{\partial p_j} \left(p_{j'} - C_1^{j'}|_{q_{j'}=D^{j'}} \right) = 0,$$

where C_1^j denotes the derivative of C^j with respect to first argument (which is the marginal cost function).

- Note that because we have already estimated the demand side, the demand functions D^j, $j = 1, \ldots, J$ and full set of demand slopes $\frac{\partial D^{j'}}{\partial p_j}$, $\forall j, j' = 1, \ldots, J$ can be calculated.

    Hence, from these J equations, we can solve for the J margins $p_j - C_1^j$. In fact, the system of equations is linear, so the solution of the marginal costs C_1^j is just,

$$\vec{c} = \vec{p} + (\Delta D)^{-1} \vec{D},$$

where c and D denote the J-vector of marginal costs and demands, and the derivative matrix ΔD is a $J \times J$ matrix where,

$$\Delta D_{(i,j)} = \begin{cases} \dfrac{\partial D^i}{\partial p_j} & \text{if models } (i,j) \text{ produced by the same firm} \\ 0 & \text{otherwise.} \end{cases}$$

The markup measures can then be obtained as $\frac{p_j - C_1^j}{p_j}$.

This is the oligopolistic equivalent of using the "inverse-elasticity" condition to calculate a monopolist's market power.

1.4.2   Estimating cost function parameters

- However, we may also be interested in estimating the coefficient in the cost function.

  If we make the further assumption that marginal costs are constant, and linear in cost components:

$$C_1^j = c^j \equiv w_j \gamma + \omega_j,$$

(where γ are parameters in the marginal cost function) then the best-response equations become

$$D^j + \sum_{j' \in K} \frac{\partial D^{j'}}{\partial p_j} \left(p_{j'} - c^j \right) = 0. \tag{1.3}$$

- This suggests a two-step approach to estimating cost parameters γ (analogous to two-step demand estimation):

  Inversion: the system of best-response Eq. (1.3) is J equation in the J unknowns c^j, $j = 1, \ldots, J$.

  IV estimation: Estimate the regression $c^j = w_j \gamma + \omega_j$. Allow for endogeneity of observed cost components w_j by using demand shifters as instruments.

  Assume you have instruments U_j such that $E(\omega U) = 0$, then find γ to minimize sample analogue $\frac{1}{J} \sum_{j=1}^{J} (c_j - w_j \gamma) U_j$.

- Naturally, you can also estimate the demand and supply side jointly: estimate (α, β, γ) all at once by jointly imposing the moment conditions $E(\xi Z) = 0$ and $E(\omega U) = 0$.

  This is not entirely straightforward, since the "dependent variables" on the supply side, the marginal costs $c^1, \ldots, c^J$, are themselves function of the demand parameters α, β. So in order to estimate jointly, we have to employ a more complicated "nested" estimation procedure which we will describe below.

1.5 Berry, Levinsohn, and Pakes (1995): Demand Estimation Using Random-coefficients Logit Model

Return to the demand side. Next we discuss the random coefficients logit model, which is the main topic of Berry, Levinsohn, and Pakes (1995).

- Assume that utility function is:

$$u_{ij} = X_j \beta_i - \alpha_i p_j + \xi_j + \epsilon_{ij}.$$

  The difference here is that the slope coefficients (α_i, β_i) are allowed to vary across households i.
- We assume that, across the population of households, the slope coefficients (α_i, β_i) are i.i.d. random variables. The most common assumption is that these random variables are jointly normally distributed:

$$(\alpha_i, \beta_i)' \sim N((\bar{\alpha}, \bar{\beta})', \Sigma).$$

  For this reason, α_i and β_i are called "random coefficients."
  Hence, $\bar{\alpha}$, $\bar{\beta}$, and Σ are additional parameters to be estimated.
- Given these assumptions, the mean utility δ_j is $X_j \bar{\beta} - \bar{\alpha} p_j + \xi_j$, and

$$u_{ij} = \delta_j + \epsilon_{ij} + (\beta_i - \bar{\beta})X_j - (\alpha_i - \bar{\alpha})p_j,$$

  so that, even if the ϵ_{ij}'s are still i.i.d. TIEV, the composite error is not. Here, the simple MNL inversion method will not work.

- The estimation methodology for this case is developed in Berry, Levinsohn, and Pakes (1995).
- First note: for a given α_i, β_i, the choice probabilities for household i take MNL form:

$$Pr(i,j) = \frac{\exp\left(X_j\beta_i - \alpha_i p_j + \xi_j\right)}{1 + \sum_{j'=1}^{J} \exp\left(X_{j'}\beta_i - \alpha_i p_{j'} + \xi_{j'}\right)}.$$

- In the whole population, the aggregate market share is just

$$
\begin{aligned}
\tilde{s}_j &= \iint Pr(i,j,)dG(\alpha_i, \beta_i) \\
&= \iint \frac{\exp\left(X_j\beta_i - \alpha_i p_j + \xi_j\right)}{1 + \sum_{j'=1}^{J} \exp\left(X_{j'}\beta_i - \alpha_i p_{j'} + \xi_{j'}\right)} dG(\alpha_i, \beta_i) \\
&= \iint \frac{\exp\left(\delta_j + (\beta_i - \bar{\beta})X_j - (\alpha_i - \bar{\alpha})p_j\right)}{1 + \sum_{j'=1}^{J} \exp\left(\delta_{j'} + (\beta_i - \bar{\beta})X_{j'} - (\alpha_i - \bar{\alpha})p_{j'}\right)} dG(\alpha_i, \beta_i) \\
&\equiv \tilde{s}_j^{RC}\left(\delta_1, \ldots, \delta_J; \bar{\alpha}, \bar{\beta}, \Sigma\right),
\end{aligned}
\tag{1.4}
$$

that is, roughly speaking, the weighted sum (where the weights are given by the probability distribution of (α, β)) of $Pr(i,j)$ across all households.

The last equation in the display above makes explicit that the predicted market share is not only a function of the mean utilities $\delta_1, \ldots, \delta_J$ (as before), but also functions of the parameters $\bar{\alpha}, \bar{\beta}, \Sigma$. Hence, the inversion step described before will not work, because the J equations matching observed to predicted shares have more than J unknowns (i.e., $\delta_1, \ldots, \delta_J; \bar{\alpha}, \bar{\beta}, \Sigma$).

Moreover, the expression in Eq. (1.4) is difficult to compute, because it is a multidimensional integral. BLP propose *simulation methods* to compute this integral. We will discuss simulation methods later. For the rest of these notes, we assume that we can compute $\tilde{s}_j^{RC}$ for every set of parameters $\bar{\alpha}, \bar{\beta}, \Sigma$.

We would like to proceed, as before, to estimate via GMM, exploiting the population moment restriction $E\left(\xi Z_m\right) = 0$, $i = 1, \ldots, M$. Let

$\theta \equiv (\bar{\alpha}, \bar{\beta}, \Sigma)$. Then the sample moment conditions are:

$$m_{m,J}(\theta) \equiv \frac{1}{J} \sum_{j=1}^{J} \left(\delta_j - X_j \bar{\beta} + \bar{\alpha} p_j \right) Z_{mj},$$

and we estimate θ by minimizing a quadratic norm in these sample moment functions:

$$\min_{\theta} Q_J(\theta) \equiv [m_{m,J}(\theta)]'_m W_J [m_{m,J}(\theta)]_m,$$

W_J is a $(M \times M)$-dimensional weighting matrix.

But problem is that we cannot perform inversion step as before, so that we cannot derive $\delta_1, \ldots, \delta_J$.

So BLP propose a "nested" estimation algorithm, with an "inner loop" nested within an "outer loop."

- In the **outer loop**, we iterate over different values of the parameters. Let $\hat{\theta}$ be the current values of the parameters being considered.
- In the **inner loop**, for the given parameter values $\hat{\theta}$, we wish to evaluate the objective function $Q(\hat{\theta})$. In order to do this, we must:

1. At current $\hat{\theta}$, we solve for the mean utilities $\delta_1(\hat{\theta}), \ldots, \delta_J(\hat{\theta})$ to solve the system of equations

$$\hat{s}_1 = \tilde{s}_1^{RC} \left(\delta_1, \ldots, \delta_J; \hat{\theta} \right)$$

$$\vdots \qquad \vdots$$

$$\hat{s}_J = \tilde{s}_J^{RC} \left(\delta_1, \ldots, \delta_J; \hat{\theta} \right).$$

Note that, since we take the parameters $\hat{\theta}$ as given, this system is J equations in the J unknowns $\delta_1(\hat{\theta}), \ldots, \delta_J(\hat{\theta})$.

2. For the resulting $\delta_1(\hat{\theta}), \ldots, \delta_J(\hat{\theta})$, calculate

$$Q(\hat{\theta}) = [m_{m,J}(\hat{\theta})]'_m W_J [m_{m,J}(\hat{\theta})]_m. \tag{1.5}$$

- Then we return to the outer loop, which searches until it finds parameter values $\hat{\theta}$ which minimize Eq. (1.5).

- Essentially, the original inversion step is now nested inside of the estimation routine.

Note that, typically, for identification, a necessary condition is that:

$$M = \dim(\vec{Z}) \geq \dim(\theta) > \dim(\alpha, \beta) = \dim([X, p]).$$

This is because there are coefficients Σ associated with the distribution of random coefficients. This implies that, even if there were no price endogeneity problem, so that (X, p) are valid instruments, we still need additional instruments in order to identify the additional parameters.[1]

Within this nested estimation procedure, we can also add a supply side to the RC model. With both demand and supply-side moment conditions, the objective function becomes:

$$Q(\theta, \gamma) = G_J(\theta, \gamma)' W_J G_J(\theta, \gamma),$$

where G_J is the $(M + N)$-dimensional vector of stacked sample moment conditions:

$$G_J(\theta, \gamma) \equiv \begin{bmatrix} \frac{1}{J} \sum_{j=1}^{J} \left(\delta_j(\theta) - X_j \bar{\beta} + \bar{\alpha} p_j \right) z_{1j} \\ \vdots \\ \frac{1}{J} \sum_{j=1}^{J} \left(\delta_j(\theta) - X_j \bar{\beta} + \bar{\alpha} p_j \right) z_{Mj} \\ \frac{1}{J} \sum_{j=1}^{J} \left(c_j(\theta) - w_j \gamma \right) u_{1j} \\ \vdots \\ \frac{1}{J} \sum_{j=1}^{J} \left(c_j(\theta) - w_j \gamma \right) u_{Nj} \end{bmatrix},$$

where M is the number of demand side IV's, and N the number of supply-side IV's. (Assuming $M + N \geq \dim(\theta) + \dim(\gamma)$.)

The only change in the estimation routine described in the previous section is that the inner loop is more complicated:

In the **inner loop**, for the given parameter values $\hat{\theta}$ and $\hat{\gamma}$, we wish to evaluate the objective function $Q(\hat{\theta}, \hat{\gamma})$. In order to do this

---

[1]See Moon, Shum, and Weidner (2012).

we must:

1. At current $\hat{\theta}$, solve for the mean utilities $\delta_1(\hat{\theta}), \ldots, \delta_J(\hat{\theta})$ as previously.
2. For the resulting $\delta_1(\hat{\theta}), \ldots, \delta_J(\hat{\theta})$, calculate

$$\vec{\tilde{s}}_j^{RC}(\hat{\theta}) \equiv \left(\tilde{s}_1^{RC}(\delta(\hat{\theta})), \ldots, \tilde{s}_J^{RC}(\delta(\hat{\theta})) \right)',$$

and also the partial derivative matrix

$$\mathbf{D}(\hat{\theta}) = \begin{pmatrix} \dfrac{\partial \tilde{s}_1^{RC}(\delta(\hat{\theta}))}{\partial p_1} & \dfrac{\partial \tilde{s}_1^{RC}(\delta(\hat{\theta}))}{\partial p_2} & \cdots & \dfrac{\partial \tilde{s}_1^{RC}(\delta(\hat{\theta}))}{\partial p_J} \\[2ex] \dfrac{\partial \tilde{s}_2^{RC}(\delta(\hat{\theta}))}{\partial p_1} & \dfrac{\partial \tilde{s}_2^{RC}(\delta(\hat{\theta}))}{\partial p_2} & \cdots & \dfrac{\partial \tilde{s}_2^{RC}(\delta(\hat{\theta}))}{\partial p_J} \\[2ex] \vdots & \vdots & \ddots & \vdots \\[2ex] \dfrac{\partial \tilde{s}_J^{RC}(\delta(\hat{\theta}))}{\partial p_1} & \dfrac{\partial \tilde{s}_J^{RC}(\delta(\hat{\theta}))}{\partial p_2} & \cdots & \dfrac{\partial \tilde{s}_J^{RC}(\delta(\hat{\theta}))}{\partial p_J} \end{pmatrix}.$$

For MNL case, these derivatives are:

$$\frac{\partial s_j}{\partial p_k} = \begin{cases} -\alpha s_j (1 - s_j) & \text{for } j = k \\ -\alpha s_j s_k & \text{for } j \neq k. \end{cases}$$

3. Use the supply-side best response equations to solve for $c_1(\hat{\theta}), \ldots, c_J(\hat{\theta})$:

$$\vec{\tilde{s}}_j^{RC}(\hat{\theta}) + \mathbf{D}(\hat{\theta}) * \begin{pmatrix} p_1 - c^1 \\ \vdots \\ p_J - c^J \end{pmatrix} = 0.$$

4. So now, you can compute $G(\hat{\theta}, \hat{\gamma})$.

1.5.1 Simulating the integral in Eq. (1.4)

The principle of simulation: approximate an expectation as a sample average. Validity is ensured by law of large numbers.

In the case of Eq. (1.4), note that in the integral there is an expectation:

$$\mathcal{E}\left(\bar{\alpha}, \bar{\beta}, \Sigma\right)$$

$$\equiv E_G \left[\frac{\exp\left(\delta_j + (\beta_i - \bar{\beta})X_j - (\alpha_i - \bar{\alpha})p_j\right)}{1 + \sum_{j'=1}^{J} \exp\left(\delta_{j'} + (\beta_i - \bar{\beta})X_{j'} - (\alpha_i - \bar{\alpha})p_{j'}\right)} \middle| \bar{\alpha}, \bar{\beta}, \Sigma \right],$$

where the random variables are α_i and β_i, which we assume to be drawn from the multivariate normal distribution $N\left((\bar{\alpha}, \bar{\beta})', \Sigma\right)$.

For $s = 1, \ldots, S$ simulation draws:

1. Draw u_1^s, u_2^s independently from N(0,1).
2. For the current parameter estimates $\hat{\bar{\alpha}}$, $\hat{\bar{\beta}}$, $\hat{\Sigma}$, transform (u_1^s, u_2^s) into a draw from $N((\hat{\bar{\alpha}}, \hat{\bar{\beta}})', \hat{\Sigma})$ using the transformation

$$\begin{pmatrix} \alpha^s \\ \beta^s \end{pmatrix} = \begin{pmatrix} \hat{\bar{\alpha}} \\ \hat{\bar{\beta}} \end{pmatrix} + \hat{\Sigma}^{1/2} \begin{pmatrix} u_1^s \\ u_2^s \end{pmatrix},$$

where $\hat{\Sigma}^{1/2}$ is shorthand for the "Cholesky factorization" of the matrix $\hat{\Sigma}$. The Cholesky factorization of a square symmetric matrix $\mathbf{\Gamma}$ is the triangular matrix $\mathbf{G}$ such that $\mathbf{G}'\mathbf{G} = \mathbf{\Gamma}$, so roughly it can be thought of as a matrix-analogue of "square root." We use the *lower triangular* version of $\hat{\Sigma}^{1/2}$.

Then approximate the integral by the sample average (over all the simulation draws)

$$\mathcal{E}\left(\hat{\bar{\alpha}}, \hat{\bar{\beta}}, \hat{\Sigma}\right) \approx \frac{1}{S} \sum_{s=1}^{S} \frac{\exp\left(\delta_j + \left(\beta^s - \hat{\bar{\beta}}\right)X_j - \left(\alpha^s - \hat{\bar{\alpha}}\right)p_j\right)}{1 + \sum_{j'=1}^{J} \exp\left(\delta_{j'} + \left(\beta^s - \hat{\bar{\beta}}\right)X_{j'} - \left(\alpha^s - \hat{\bar{\alpha}}\right)p_{j'}\right)}.$$

For given $\hat{\bar{\alpha}}, \hat{\bar{\beta}}, \hat{\Sigma}$, the law of large numbers ensure that this approximation is accurate as $S \to \infty$.

(Results: Marginal costs and markups from BLP paper.)

1.6 Applications

Applications of this methodology have been voluminous. Here we discuss just a few.

1. Evaluation of voluntary export restraints (VERs): In Berry, Levinsohn, and Pakes (1999), this methodology is applied to evaluate the effects of VERs. These were voluntary quotas that the Japanese auto manufacturers abided by and which restricted their exports to the United States during the 1980's.

The VERs do not affect the demand-side, but only the supply-side. Namely, firm profits are given by:

$$\pi_k = \sum_{j \in \mathcal{K}} (p_j - c_j - \lambda \text{VER}_k) D^j.$$

In the above, VER_k are dummy variables for whether firm k is subject to VER (so whether firm k is Japanese firm). VER is modeled as an "implicit tax," with $\lambda \geq 0$ functioning as a per-unit tax: if $\lambda = 0$, then the VER has no effect on behavior, while $\lambda > 0$ implies that VER is having an effect similar to increase in marginal cost c_j. The coefficient λ is an additional parameter to be estimated, on the supply-side.

(Results: Effects of VER on firm profits and consumer welfare.)

2. Welfare from new goods, and merger evaluation: After cost function parameters γ are estimated, you can simulate equilibrium prices under alternative market structures, such as mergers, or entry (or exit) of firms or goods. These counterfactual prices are valid assuming that consumer preferences and firms' cost functions don't change as market structures change. Petrin (2002) presents consumer welfare benefits from introduction of the minivan, and Nevo (2001) presents merger simulation results for the ready-to-eat cereal industry.

3. Geographic differentiation: In our description of BLP model, we assume that all consumer heterogeneity is unobserved. Some models have considered types of consumer heterogeneity where the marginal distribution of the heterogeneity in the population is observed. In BLP's original paper, they include household income in the utility functions, and integrate out over the population income distribution (from the Current Population Survey) in simulating the predicted market shares.

Another important example of this type of observed consumer heterogeneity is consumers' location. The idea is that the products are geographically differentiated, so that consumers might prefer choices which are located closer to their home. Assume you want to model competition among movie theaters, as in Davis (2006). The utility of consumer i from theater j is:

$$U_{ij} = -\alpha p_j + \beta(L_i - L_j) + \xi_j + \epsilon_{ij},$$

where $(L_i - L_j)$ denotes the geographic distance between the locations of consumer I and theater j. The predicted market shares for each theater can be calculated by integrating out over the marginal empirical population density (i.e., integrating over the distribution of L_i). See also Thomadsen (2005) for a model of the fast-food industry, and Houde (2012) for retail gasoline markets. The latter paper is noteworthy because instead of integrating over the marginal distribution of where people live, Houde integrates over the distribution of commuting routes. He argues that consumers are probably more sensitive to a gasoline station's location relative to their driving routes, rather than relative to their homes.

1.7 Additional Details: General Presentation of Random Utility Models

Introduce the *social surplus function*

$$H(\vec{U}) \equiv \mathbb{E}\left\{\max_{j \in \mathcal{J}}(U_j + \epsilon_j)\right\},$$

where the expectation is taken over some joint distribution of $(\epsilon_1, \ldots, \epsilon_J)$.

For each $\lambda \in [0, 1]$, for all values of $\vec{\epsilon}$, and for any two vectors $\vec{U}$ and $\vec{U'}$, we have

$$\max_j(\lambda U_j + (1 - \lambda)U'_j + \epsilon_j) \leq \lambda \max_j(U_j + \epsilon_j) + (1 - \lambda)\max_j(U'_j + \epsilon_j).$$

Since this holds for all vectors $\vec{\epsilon}$, it also holds in expectation, so that

$$H(\lambda\vec{U} + (1 - \lambda)\vec{U'}) \leq \lambda H(\vec{U}) + (1 - \lambda)H(\vec{U'}).$$

That is, $H(\cdot)$ is a convex function. We consider its *Fenchel–Legendre transformation*[2] defined as

$$H^*(\vec{p}) = \max_{\vec{U}}(\vec{p} \cdot \vec{U} - H(\vec{U})),$$

where $\vec{p}$ is some J-dimensional vector of choice probabilities. Because H is convex, we have that the FOCs characterizing H^* are

$$\vec{p} = \nabla_{\vec{U}} H(\vec{U}). \tag{1.6}$$

Note that for discrete-choice models, this function is many-to-one. For any constant k, $H(\vec{U} + k) = H(\vec{U}) + k$, and hence if $\vec{U}$ satisfies $\vec{p} = \nabla_{\vec{U}} H(\vec{U})$, then also $\vec{p} = \nabla_{\vec{U}} H(\vec{U} + k)$.

$H^*(\cdot)$ is also called the "conjugate" function of $H(\cdot)$. Furthermore, it turns out that the conjugate function of $H^*(\vec{p})$ is just $H(\vec{U})$ — for this reason, the functions H^* and H have a dual relationship, and

$$H(\vec{U}) = \max_{\vec{p}}(\vec{p} \cdot \vec{U} - H^*(\vec{p}))$$

with,

$$\vec{U} \in \partial_{\vec{p}} H^*(\vec{p}), \tag{1.7}$$

where $\partial_{\vec{p}} H^*(\vec{p})$ denotes the *subdifferential* (or, synonymously, subgradiant or subderivative) of H^* at $\vec{p}$. For discrete choice models, this is typically a multivalued mapping (a correspondence) because $\nabla H(\vec{U})$ is many-to-one.[3] In the discrete choice literature, Eq. (1.6) is called the William–Daly–Zachary theorem, and analogous to the Shepard/Hotelling lemmas, for the random utility model. Equation (1.7) is a precise statement of the "inverse mapping" from choice probabilities to utilities for discrete choice models, and thus

---

[2]See Gelfand and Fomin (1965), Rockafellar (1971), Chiong, Galichon, and Shum (2013).

[3]Indeed, in the special case where $\nabla H(\cdot)$ is one-to-one, then we have $\vec{U} = (\nabla H(\vec{p}))$. This is the case of the classical Legendre transform.

reformulates (and is a more general statement of) the "inversion" result in Berry (1994) and Berry, Levinshon, and Pakes (1995).

For specific assumptions on the joint distribution of $\vec{\epsilon}$ (as with the generalized extreme value case cited previously), we can derive a closed form for the social surplus function $H(\vec{U})$, which immediately yield the choice probabilities via Eq. (1.6) above.

For the MNL model, we know that

$$H(\vec{U}) = \log\left(\sum_{i=0}^{K} \exp(U_i)\right).$$

From the conjugacy relation, we know that $\vec{p} = \nabla H(\vec{U})$. Normalizing $U_0 = 0$, this leads to $U_i = \log(p_i/p_0)$ for $i = 1, \ldots, K$. Plugging this back into the definition of $H^*(\vec{p})$, we get that,

$$H^*(\vec{p}) = \sum_{i'=0}^{K} p_{i'} \log(p_{i'}/p_0) - \log\left(\frac{1}{p_0}\sum_{i'=0}^{K} p_{i'}\right) \tag{1.8}$$

$$= \sum_{i'=1}^{K} p_{i'} \log p_{i'} - \log p_0 \sum_{i'=1}^{K} p_{i'} + \log p_0 \tag{1.9}$$

$$= \sum_{i'=0}^{K} p_{i'} \log p_{i'}. \tag{1.10}$$

To confirm, we again use the conjugacy relation $\vec{U} = \nabla H^*(\vec{p})$ to get (for $i = 0, 1, \ldots, K$) that $U_i = \log p_i$. Then imposing the normalization $U_0 = 0$, we get that $U_i = \log(p_i/p_0)$.

Bibliography

Bajari, P. and L. Benkard (2005): "Demand Estimation With Heterogeneous Consumers and Unobserved Product Characteristics: A Hedonic Approach," *J. Polit. Econ.*, **113**, 1239–1276.

Berry, S. (1994): "Estimating Discrete Choice Models of Product Differentiation," *RAND J. Econ.*, **25**, 242–262.

Berry, S., J. Levinsohn and A. Pakes (1995): "Automobile Prices in Market Equilibrium," *Econometrica*, **63**, 841–890.

Berry, S., J. Levinsohn and A. Pakes (1999): "Voluntary Export Restraints on Automobiles: Evaluating a Strategic Trade Policy," *Am. Econ. Rev.*, **89**, 400–430.

Bresnahan, T. (1989): "Empirical Studies of Industries with Market Power," in *Handbook of Industrial Organization*, eds. by R. Schmalensee and R. Willig, vol. 2. North-Holland.

Chiong, K., A. Galichon and M. Shum (2013): "Duality in Dynamic Discrete Choice Models," mimeo, Caltech.

Davis, P. (2006): "Spatial Competition in Retail Markets: Movie Theaters," *RAND J. Econ.*, 964–982.

Gelfand, I. and S. Fomin (1965): *Calculus of Variations*. Dover.

Goldberg, P. (1995): "Product Differentiation and Oligopoly in International Markets: The Case of the US Automobile Industry," *Econometrica*, **63**, 891–951.

Hausman, J. (1996): "Valuation of New Goods under Perfect and Imperfect Competition," in *The Economics of New Goods*, eds. by T. Bresnahan and R. Gordon, pp. 209–237. University of Chicago Press.

Houde, J. (2012): "Spatial Differentiation and Vertical Mergers in Retail Markets for Gasoline," *Am. Econ. Rev.*, **102**, 2147–2182.

Keane, M. (1994): "A Computationally Practical Simulation Estimator for Panel Data," *Econometrica*, **62**, 95–116.

Maddala, G. S. (1983): *Limited-dependent and Qualitative Variables in Econometrics*. Cambridge University Press.

McFadden, D. (1978): "Modelling the Choice of Residential Location," in *Spatial Interaction Theory and Residential Location*, ed. by A. K. North. Holland.

McFadden, D. (1981): "Statistical Models for Discrete Panel Data," in *Econometric Models of Probabilistic Choice*, eds. C. Manski and D. McFadden. MIT Press.

McFadden, D. (1989): "A Method of Simulated Moments for Estimation of Discrete Response Models without Numerical Integration," *Econometrica*, **57**, 995–1026.

Moon, R., M. Shum and M. Weidner (2012): "Estimation of Random Coefficients Logit Demand Models with Interactive Fixed Effects," manuscript. University of Southern California.

Nevo, A. (2001): "Measuring Market Power in the Ready-to-eat Cereals Industry," *Econometrica*, **69**, 307–342.

Petrin, A. (2002): "Quantifying the Benefits of New Products: the Case of the Minivan," *J. Polit. Econ.*, **110**, 705–729.

Rockafellar, T. (1971): *Convex Analysis*. Princeton University Press.

Rosen, S. (1974): "Hedonic Prices and Implicit Markets: Product Differentiation in Pure Competition," *J. Polit. Econ.*, **82**, 34–55.

Thomadsen, R. (2005): "The Effect of Ownership Structure on Prices in Geographically Differentiated Industries," *RAND J. Econ.*, 908–929.

Trajtenberg, M. (1989): "The Welfare Analysis of Product Innovations, with an Application to Computed Tomography Scanners," *J. Polit. Econ.*, **97**(2), 444–479.

Chapter 2

Single-agent Dynamic Models: Part 1

In these lecture notes, we consider specification and estimation of dynamic optimization models. Focus on single-agent models.

2.1 Rust (1987)

Rust (1987) is one of the first papers in this literature. Model is quite simple, but empirical framework introduced in this Chapter for dynamic discrete-choice (DDC) models is still widely applied.

Agent is Harold Zurcher (HZ), Manager of bus depot in Madison, Wisconsin. Each week, HZ must decide whether to replace the bus engine, or keep it running for another week. This engine replacement problem is an example of an *optimal stopping* problem, which features the usual tradeoff: (i) there are large fixed costs associated with "stopping" (replacing the engine), but new engine has lower associated future maintenance costs; (ii) by not replacing the engine, you avoid the fixed replacement costs, but suffer higher future maintenance costs.

2.1.1 Behavioral model

At the end of each week t, HZ decides whether or not to replace engine. *Control* variable defined as:

$$i_t = \begin{cases} 1 & \text{if HZ replaces} \\ 0 & \text{otherwise.} \end{cases}$$

For simplicity, we describe the case where there is only one bus (in the Chapter, buses are treated as independent entities).

HZ chooses the (infinite) sequence $\{i_1, i_2, i_3, \ldots, i_t, i_{t+1}, \ldots\}$ to maximize discounted expected utility stream:

$$\max_{\{i_1, i_2, i_3, \ldots, i_t, i_{t+1}, \ldots\}} E \sum_{t=1}^{\infty} \beta^{t-1} u\left(x_t, \epsilon_t, i_t; \theta\right), \qquad (2.1)$$

where

- The *state* variables of this problem are:
  1. x_t: the mileage. Both HZ and the econometrician observe this, so we call this the "observed state variable,"
  2. ϵ_t: the utility shocks. Econometrician does not observe this, so we call it the "unobserved state variable."

- x_t is the mileage of the bus at the end of week t. Assume that evolution of mileage is stochastic (from HZ's point of view) and follows

$$x_{t+1} \begin{cases} \sim G(x'|x_t) & \text{if } i_t = 0 \text{ (don't replace engine in period } t) \\ \sim G(x'|0) & \text{if } i_t = 1 \text{: once replaced, mileage gets} \\ & \qquad \text{reset to zero,} \end{cases}$$

$$(2.2)$$

and $G(x'|x)$ is the conditional probability distribution of next period's mileage x' given that current mileage is x. HZ knows G; econometrician knows the form of G, up to a vector of parameters which are estimated.[1]

- ϵ_t denotes shocks in period t, which affect HZ's choice of whether to replace the engine. These are the "structural errors" of the model (they are observed by HZ, but not by us), and we will discuss them in more detail below.

---

[1]Since mileage evolves randomly, this implies that even given a sequence of replacement choices $\{i_1, i_2, i_3, \ldots, i_t, i_{t+1}, \ldots\}$, the corresponding sequence of mileages $\{x_1, x_2, x_3, \ldots, x_t, x_{t+1}, \ldots\}$ is still random. The expectation in Eq. (2.1) is over this stochastic sequence of mileages and over the shocks $\{\epsilon_1, \epsilon_2, \ldots\}$.

Define value function:

$$V(x_t, \epsilon_t) = \max_{i_\tau,\ \tau=t+1,t+2,\ldots} E_t \left[\sum_{\tau=t+1}^{\infty} \beta^{\tau-t} u(x_t, \epsilon_t, i_t; \theta) \,|x_t \right],$$

where maximum is over all possible sequences of $\{i_{t+1}, i_{t+2}, \ldots\}$. Note that we have imposed stationarity, so that the value function $V(\cdot)$ is a function of t only indirectly, through the value that the state variable x takes during period t.[2]

Using the Bellman equation, we can break down the DO problem into an (infinite) sequence of single-period decisions:

$$i_t = i^*(x_t, \epsilon_t; \theta) = \operatorname{argmax}_i \left\{ u(x_t, \epsilon_t, i; \theta) + \beta E_{x',\epsilon'|x_t,\epsilon_t,i_t} V(x', \epsilon') \right\},$$

where the value function is

$$
\begin{aligned}
V(x, \epsilon) &= \max_{i=1,0} \left\{ u(x, \epsilon, i; \theta) + \beta E_{x',\epsilon'|x_t,\epsilon_t,i_t} V(x', \epsilon') \right\} \\
&= \max \left\{ u(x, \epsilon, 0; \theta) + \beta E_{x',\epsilon'|x_t,\epsilon_t,i_t=0} V(x', \epsilon'), u(x, \epsilon, 1; \theta) \right. \\
&\qquad \left. + \beta E_{x',\epsilon'|0,\epsilon_t,i_t=1} V(x', \epsilon'). \right\} \\
&= \max \{ \tilde{V}(x, \epsilon, 1), \tilde{V}(x, \epsilon, 0) \}. \qquad (2.3)
\end{aligned}
$$

In the above, we define the **choice-specific value function**

$$
\tilde{V}(x, \epsilon, i) = \begin{cases} u(x, \epsilon, 1; \theta) + \beta E_{x',\epsilon'|x=0,\epsilon,i=1} V(x', \epsilon') & \text{if } i = 1, \\ u(x, \epsilon, 0; \theta) + \beta E_{x',\epsilon'|x,\epsilon,i=0} V(x', \epsilon') & \text{if } i = 0. \end{cases}
$$

We make the following parametric assumptions on utility flow:

$$u(x_t, \epsilon_t, i; \theta) = -c\big((1 - i_t) * x_t; \theta\big) - i * RC + \epsilon_{it},$$

where,

- $c(\cdots)$ is the maintenance cost function, which is presumably increasing in x (higher x means higher costs).

---

[2] An important distinction between empirical papers with dynamic optimization models is whether agents have infinite-horizon, or finite-horizon. Stationarity (or time homogeneity) is assumed for infinite-horizon problems, and they are solved using value function iteration. Finite-horizon problems are nonstationary, and solved by backward induction starting from the final period.

- RC denotes the "lumpy" fixed costs of adjustment. The presence of these costs implies that HZ would not want to replace the engine every period.
- ϵ_{it}, $i = 0, 1$ are structural errors, which represents factors which affect HZ's replacement choice i_t in period t, but are unobserved by the econometrician. Define $\epsilon_t \equiv (\epsilon_{0t}, \epsilon_{1t})$.

  As Rust remarks (1987), you need this in order to generate a positive likelihood for your observed data. Without these ϵ's, we observe as much as HZ does, and $i_t = i^*(x_t; \theta)$, so that replacement decision should be perfectly explained by mileage. Hence, model will not be able to explain situations where there are two periods with identical mileage, but in one period HZ replaced, and in the other HZ doesn't replace. (Tension between this empirical practice and "falsifiability: of model")

As remarked earlier, these assumptions imply a very simple type of optimal decision rule $i^*(x, \epsilon; \theta)$: in any period t, you replace when $x_t \geq x^*(\epsilon_t)$, where $x^*(\epsilon_t)$ is some optimal cutoff mileage level, which depends on the value of the shocks ϵ_t.

Parameters to be estimated are:

1. Parameters of maintenance cost function $c(\cdots)$;
2. Replacement cost RC;
3. Parameters of mileage transition function $G(x'|x)$.

Remark: Distinguishing myopic from forward-looking behavior. In these models, the discount factor β is typically not estimated. Essentially, the time series data on $\{i_t, x_t\}$ could be equally well explained by a myopic model, which posits that

$$i_t = \mathrm{argmax}_{i \in \{0,1\}} \{u(x_t, \epsilon_t, i)\}$$

or a forward-looking model, which posits that

$$i_t = \mathrm{argmax}_{i \in \{0,1\}} \{\tilde{V}(x_t, \epsilon_t, i)\}.$$

In both models, the choice i_t depends just on the current state variables x_t, ϵ_t. Indeed, Magnac and Thesmar (2002) show that in general, DDC models are nonparametrically underidentified, without knowledge of β and $F(\epsilon)$, the distribution of the ϵ shocks. (Below, we show how knowledge of β and F, along with an additional normalization, permits nonparametric identification of the utility functions in this model.)

Intuitively, in this model, it is difficult to identify β apart from fixed costs. In this model, if HZ were myopic (i.e., β close to zero) and replacement costs RC were low, his decisions may look similar as when he were forward-looking (i.e., β close to 1) and RC were large. Reduced-form tests for forward-looking behavior exploit scenarios in which some variables which affect future utility are known in period t: consumers are deemed forward-looking if their period t decisions depends on these variables. Examples: Chevalier and Goolsbee (2009) examine whether students' choices of purchasing a textbook now depend on the possibility that a new edition will be released soon. Becker, Grossman, and Murphy (1994) argue that cigarette addiction is "rational" by showing that cigarette consumption is response to permanent future changes in cigarette prices.

2.1.2 Econometric model

Data: observe $\{i_t, x_t\}$, $t = 1, \ldots, T$ for 62 buses. Treat buses as homogeneous and independent (i.e., replacement decision on bus j is not affected by replacement decision on bus j').

Rust makes the following conditional independence assumption, on the Markovian transition probabilities in the Bellman equation above:

Assumption 1. $(x_t, \vec{\epsilon}_t)$ *is a stationary controlled first-order Markov process, with transition*

$$p(x', \epsilon' | x, \epsilon, i) = p(\epsilon' | x', x, \epsilon, i) \cdot p(x' | x, e, i)$$
$$= p(\epsilon' | x') \cdot p(x' | x, i). \tag{2.4}$$

The first line is just factoring the joint density into a conditional times marginal. The second line shows the simplifications from Rust's assumptions. Namely, two types of conditional independence: (i) given

x, ϵ's are independent over time; and (ii) conditional on x and i, x' is independent of ϵ.

Likelihood function for a single bus:

$$l\left(x_1, \ldots, x_T, i_1, \ldots, i_T | x_0, i_0; \theta\right)$$

$$= \prod_{t=1}^{T} \text{Prob}\left(i_t, x_t | x_0, i_0, \ldots, x_{t-1}, i_{t-1}; \theta\right)$$

$$= \prod_{t=1}^{T} \text{Prob}\left(i_t, x_t | x_{t-1}, i_{t-1}; \theta\right)$$

$$= \prod_{t=1}^{T} \text{Prob}\left(i_t | x_t; \theta\right) \times \text{Prob}\left(x_t | x_{t-1}, i_{t-1}; \theta_3\right). \qquad (2.5)$$

Both the third and fourth lines arise from the conditional independence assumption. Note that, in the dynamic optimization problem, the optimal choice of i_t depends on the state variables (x_t, ϵ_t). Hence the third line (implying that $\{x_t, i_t\}$ evolves as first-order Markov) relies on the conditional serial independence of ϵ_t. The last equality also arises from this conditional serial independence assumption.

Hence, the log-likelihood is additively separable in the two components:

$$\log l = \sum_{t=1}^{T} \log \text{Prob}\left(i_t | x_t; \theta\right) + \sum_{t=1}^{T} \log \text{Prob}\left(x_t | x_{t-1}, i_{t-1}; \theta_3\right).$$

Here $\theta_3 \subset \theta$ denotes the subset of parameters which enter G, the transition probability function for mileage. Because $\theta_3 \subset \theta$, we can maximize the likelihood function above in two steps.

First step: Estimate θ_3, the parameters of the Markov transition probabilities for mileage. We assume a discrete distribution for mileage x, taking K distinct and equally-spaced values $\{x_{[1]}, x_{[2]}, \ldots, x_{[K]}\}$, in increasing order, where $x_{[k']} - x_{[k]} = \Delta \cdot (k' - k)$, where Δ is a mileage increment (Rust considers $\Delta = 5{,}000$). Also assume that given the current state $x_t = x_{[k]}$, the mileage in the next period can move up to at most $x_{[k+J]}$. (When $i_t = 1$; so that engine is replaced, we reset $x_t = 0 = x_{[0]}$.) Then the mileage transition probabilities can be expressed as:

$$P(x_{[k+j]}|x_{[k]}, d = 0) = \begin{cases} p_j & \text{if } 0 \leq j \leq J, \\ 0 & \text{otherwise}, \end{cases} \qquad (2.6)$$

so that $\theta_3 \equiv \{p_0, p_1, \ldots, p_J\}$, with $0 < p_0, \ldots, p_J < 1$ and $\sum_{j=1}^{J} p_j = 1$.

This first step can be executed separately from the substantial second step. θ_3 estimated just by empirical frequencies: $\hat{p}_j = \text{freq}\{x_{t+1} - x_t = \Delta \cdot j\}$, for all $0 \leq j \leq J$.

Second step: Estimate the remaining parameters $\theta\backslash\theta_3$, parameters of maintenance cost function $c(\cdots)$ and engine replacement costs.

Here, we make a further assumption:

Assumption 2. *The ϵ's are identically and independently distributed* (i.i.d.) *(across choices and periods), according to the Type I extreme value distribution. So this implies that in Eq. (2.4) above, $p(\epsilon'|x') = p(\epsilon')$, for all x'.*

Expand the expression for $\text{Prob}(i_t = 1|x_t; \theta)$ equals

$$\text{Prob}\{-c(0;\theta) - RC + \epsilon_{1t} + \beta E_{x',\epsilon'|0}V(x', \epsilon')$$
$$> -c(x_t;\theta) + \epsilon_{0t} + \beta E_{x',\epsilon'|x_t}V(x', \epsilon')\}$$
$$= \text{Prob}\{\epsilon_{1t} - \epsilon_{0t} > c(0;\theta) - c(x_t;\theta)$$
$$+ \beta\left[E_{x',\epsilon'|x_t}V(x, \epsilon) - E_{x',\epsilon'|0}V(x', \epsilon')\right] + RC\}.$$

Because of the logit assumptions on ϵ_t, the replacement probability simplifies to a multinomial logit-like expression:

$$= \frac{\exp\left(-c(0;\theta) - RC + \beta E_{x',\epsilon'|x_t=0}V(x', \epsilon')\right)}{\exp\left(-c(0;\theta) - RC + \beta E_{x',\epsilon'|x_t=0}V(x', \epsilon')\right)}.$$
$$+ \exp\left(-c(x_t;\theta) + \beta E_{x',\epsilon'|x_t}V(x', \epsilon')\right)$$

This is called a "dynamic logit" model, in the literature.

Defining $\bar{u}(x,i;\theta) \equiv u(x,\epsilon,i;\theta) - \epsilon_i$ the choice probability takes the form

$$\text{Prob}\,(i_t|x_t;\theta) = \frac{\exp\left(\bar{u}(x_t,i_t,\theta) + \beta E_{x',\epsilon'|x_t,i_t} V(x',\epsilon')\right)}{\sum_{i=0,1} \exp\left(\bar{u}(x_t,i,\theta) + \beta E_{x',\epsilon'|x_t,i} V(x',\epsilon')\right)}.$$

(2.7)

Estimation method for second step: Nested fixed-point algorithm

The second-step of the estimation procedures is via a "nested fixed point algorithm."

Outer loop: search over different parameter values $\hat{\theta}$.

Inner loop: For $\hat{\theta}$, we need to compute the value function $V(x,\epsilon;\hat{\theta})$. After $V(x,\epsilon;\hat{\theta})$ is obtained, we can compute the LL fxn in Eq. (2.7).

Computational details for inner loop

Compute value function $V(x,\epsilon;\hat{\theta})$ by iterating over Bellman's equation (2.3).

A clever and computationally convenient feature in Rust's paper is that he iterates over the *expected* value function $EV(x,i) \equiv E_{x',\epsilon'|x,i} V(x',\epsilon';\theta)$. The reason for this is that you avoid having to calculate the value function at values of ϵ_0 and ϵ_1, which are additional state variables. He iterates over the following equation (which is Eq. (4.14) in his paper):

$$EV(x,i) = \int_y \log\left\{ \sum_{j \in C(y)} \exp\left[\bar{u}(y,j;\theta) + \beta EV(y,j)\right] \right\} p(dy|x,i).$$

(2.8)

Somewhat awkward notation: here "EV" denotes a function. Here x,i denotes the *previous* period's mileage and replacement choice, and y,j denote the *current* period's mileage and choice (as will be clear below).

This equation can be derived from Bellman's Equation (2.3):

$$V(y, \epsilon; \theta) = \max_{j \in 0,1} [\bar{u}(y, j; \theta) + \epsilon + \beta EV(y, j)]$$

$$\Rightarrow E_{y,\epsilon}[V(y, \epsilon; \theta) \mid x, i] \equiv EV(x, i; \theta)$$

$$= E_{y,\epsilon|x,i} \left\{ \max_{j \in 0,1} [\bar{u}(y, j; \theta) + \epsilon + \beta EV(y, j)] \right\}$$

$$= E_{y|x,i} E_{\epsilon|y,x,i} \left\{ \max_{j \in 0,1} [\bar{u}(y, j; \theta) + \epsilon + \beta EV(y, j)] \right\}$$

$$= E_{y|x,i} \log \left\{ \sum_{j=0,1} \exp [\bar{u}(y, j; \theta) + \beta EV(y, j)] \right\}$$

$$= \int_y \log \left\{ \sum_{j=0,1} \exp [\bar{u}(y, j; \theta) + \beta EV(y, j)] \right\} p(dy|x, i).$$

The next-to-last equality uses the closed-form expression for the expectation of the maximum, for extreme-value variates.[3]

Once the $EV(x, i; \theta)$ function is computed for θ, the choice probabilities $p(i_t|x_t)$ can be constructed as

$$\frac{\exp (\bar{u}(x_t, i_t; \theta) + \beta EV(x_t, i_t; \theta))}{\sum_{i=0,1} \exp (\bar{u}(x_t, i; \theta) + \beta EV(x_t, i; \theta))}.$$

The value iteration procedure: The expected value function $EV(\cdots; \theta)$ will be computed for each value of the parameters θ. The computational procedure is iterative.

Let τ index the iterations. Let $EV^\tau(x, i)$ denote the expected value function during the τth iteration. (We suppress the functional dependence of EV on θ for convenience.) Here, Rust assumes that mileage is discrete- (finite-) valued, and takes K values, each spaced 5,000 miles apart, consistently with earlier modeling of mileage transition function in Eq. (2.6). Let the values of the state variable x be discretized into a grid of points, which we denote $\vec{r}$.

---

[3]See Chiong, Galichon, and Shum (2013) for the most general treatment of this.

Because of this assumption that x is discrete, the $EV(x, i)$ function is now finite dimensional, having $2 \times K$ elements.

- $\tau = 0$: Start from an initial guess of the expected value function $EV(x, i)$. Common way is to start with $EV(x, i) = 0$, for all $x \in \vec{r}$, and $i = 0, 1$.
- $\tau = 1$: Use Eq. (2.8) and $EV^0(x; \theta)$ to calculate, at each $x \in \vec{r}$, and $i \in \{0, 1\}$.

$$EV^1(x, i) = \sum_{y \in \vec{r}} \log \left\{ \sum_{j \in C(y)} \exp \left[\bar{u}(y, j; \theta) + \beta EV^0(y, j) \right] \right\} p(y|x, i),$$

where the transition probabilities $p(y|x, i)$ are given by Eq. (2.6) above.

Now check: is $EV^1(x, i)$ close to $EV^0(x, i)$? Check whether

$$\sup_{x, i} |EV^1(x, i) - EV^0(x, i)| < \eta,$$

where η is some very small number (e.g., 0.0001). If so, then you are done. If not, then go to next iteration $\tau = 2$.

Bibliography

Becker, G., M. Grossman and K. Murphy (1994): "An Empirical Analysis of Cigarette Addiction," *Am. Econ. Rev.*, **84**, 396–418.

Chevalier, J. and A. Goolsbee (2009): "Are Durable Goods Consumers Forward Looking? Evidence from the College Textbook Market," *Q. J. Econ.*, **124**, 1853–1884.

Chiong, K., A. Galichon and M. Shum (2013): "Duality in Dynamic Discrete Choice Models," mimeo, Caltech.

Magnac, T. and D. Thesmar (2002): "Identifying Dynamic Discrete Decision Processes," *Econometrica*, **70**, 801–816.

Rust, J. (1987): "Optimal Replacement of GMC Bus Engines: An Empirical Model of Harold Zurcher," *Econometrica*, **55**, 999–1033.

Chapter 3

Single-agent Dynamic Models: Part 2

3.1 Alternative Estimation Approaches: Estimating Dynamic Optimization Models Without Numeric Dynamic Programming

One problem with Rust approach to estimating dynamic discrete-choice (DDC) model is, it is very computer intensive. It requires using numeric dynamic programming (DP) to compute the value function(s) for every parameter vector θ.

Here we discuss an alternative method of estimation, which avoids explicit DP. Present main ideas and motivation using a simplified version of Hotz and Miller (1993), Hotz *et al.* (1994). For simplicity, think about Harold Zurcher (HZ) model. What do we observe in data from DDC framework? For bus j, time t, observe:

- $\{x_{jt}, i_{jt}\}$: observed state variables x_{jt} and discrete decision (control) variable i_{jt}.

    Let $j = 1, \ldots, N$ index the buses, $t = 1, \ldots, T$ index the time periods.

- For HZ model: x_{jt} is mileage since last replacement on bus i in period t, and i_{jt} is whether or not engine of bus j was replaced in period t.

- Unobserved state variables: ϵ_{jt}, identically and independently distributed (i.i.d.) over j and t. Assume that distribution is known (Type 1 Extreme Value in Rust model).

3.1.1 Notation: Hats and Tildes

In the following, let quantities with hats ˆ's denote objects obtained just from data.

Objects with tildes ˜'s denote "predicted" quantities, obtained from both data and calculated from model given parameter values θ.

Hats: From this data alone, we can estimate (or "identify"):

- Choice probabilities, conditional on state variable: Prob $(i = 1|x),$[1] estimated by,

$$\hat{P}(i=1|x) \equiv \sum_{i=1}^{N}\sum_{t=1}^{T} \frac{1}{\sum_i \sum_t \mathbf{1}\left(x_{jt}=x\right)} \cdot \mathbf{1}\left(i_{jt}=1, x_{jt}=x\right).$$

  Since Prob$(i=0|x) = 1 - \text{Prob}(i=1|x)$, we have $\hat{P}(i=0|x) = 1 - \hat{P}(i=1|x)$.
- Transition probabilities of observed state and control variables: $G(x'|x,i),$[2] estimated by conditional empirical distribution

$$\hat{G}(x'|x,i) \equiv \begin{cases} \displaystyle\sum_{i=1}^{N}\sum_{t=1}^{T-1} \frac{1}{\sum_i \sum_t \mathbf{1}\left(x_{jt}=x, i_{jt}=0\right)} \\ \quad \cdot \mathbf{1}\left(x_{j,t+1} \leq x', x_{jt}=x, i_{jt}=0\right) & \text{if } i=0, \\[2em] \displaystyle\sum_{i=1}^{N}\sum_{t=1}^{T-1} \frac{1}{\sum_i \sum_t \mathbf{1}\left(i_{jt}=1\right)} \\ \quad \cdot \mathbf{1}\left(x_{j,t+1} \leq x', i_{jt}=1\right) & \text{if } i=1. \end{cases}$$

- In practice, when x is continuous, we estimate smoothed version of these functions by introducing a "smoothing weight" $w_{jt} = w(x_{jt}; x)$ such that $\sum_j \sum_t w_{jt} = 1$. Then, for instance, the choice

---

[1] By stationarity, note we do not index this probability explicitly with time t.
[2] By stationarity, note we do not index the G function explicitly with time t.

probability is approximated by

$$\hat{p}(i = 1|x) = \sum_j \sum_t w_{jt} \mathbf{1}(i_{jt} = 1).$$

One possibility for the weights is a kernel-weighting function. Consider a kernel function $k(\cdot)$ which is symmetric around 0 and integrates to 1. Then

$$w_{jt} = \frac{k\left(\frac{x_{jt}-x}{h}\right)}{\sum_{j'}\sum_{t'} k\left(\frac{x_{j't'}-x}{h}\right)},$$

h is a bandwidth. Note that as $h \to 0$, then $w_{it} \to \frac{\mathbf{1}(x_{jt}=x)}{\sum_{j'}\sum_{t'}\mathbf{1}(x_{j't'}=x)}$.

Tildes and forward simulation: Let $\tilde{V}(x, i; \theta)$ denote the choice-specific value function, minus the error term ϵ_i.

With estimates of $\hat{G}(\cdot|\cdot)$ and $\hat{p}(\cdot|\cdot)$, as well as a parameter vector θ, you can "estimate" these choice-specific value functions by exploiting an alternative representation of value function: letting i^* denote the optimal sequence of decisions, we have:

$$V(x_t, \epsilon_t) = \mathbb{E}\left[\sum_{\tau=0}^{\infty} \beta_{\tau t}\left\{u(x_\tau, i_t^*) + \epsilon_{i_t^*}\right\} \cdot |x_t, \epsilon_t\right].$$

This implies that the choice-specific value functions can be obtained by constructing the sum[3]

$$\tilde{V}(x, i = 1; \theta) = u(x, i = 1; \theta) + \beta \mathbb{E}_{x'|x,i=1}\mathbb{E}_{i'|x'}\mathbb{E}_{\epsilon'|i',x'}\left[u(x', i'; \theta) + \epsilon_{i'}'\right.$$

$$\left. + \beta\mathbb{E}_{x''|x',i'}\mathbb{E}_{i''|x''}\mathbb{E}_{\epsilon'|i'',x''}\left[u(x'', i''; \theta) + \epsilon_{i''}'' + \beta\cdots\right]\right],$$

$$\tilde{V}(x, i = 0; \theta) = u(x, i = 0; \theta) + \beta \mathbb{E}_{x'|x,i=0}\mathbb{E}_{i'|x'}\mathbb{E}_{\epsilon'|i',x'}\left[u(x', i'; \theta) + \epsilon_{i'}'\right.$$

$$\left. + \beta\mathbb{E}_{x''|x',i'}\mathbb{E}_{i''|x''}\mathbb{E}_{\epsilon'|i'',x''}\left[u(x'', i''; \theta) + \epsilon_{i''}'' + \beta\cdots\right]\right].$$

Here $u(x, i; \theta)$ denotes the per-period utility of taking choice i at state x, *without* the additive logit error. Note that the knowledge of $i'|x'$

---

[3]Note that the distribution $(x', i', \epsilon'|x, i)$ can be factored, via the conditional independence assumption, into $(\epsilon'|i', x')(i'|x')(x'|x, i)$.

is crucial to being able to forward-simulate the choice-specific value functions. Otherwise, $i'|x'$ is multinomial with probabilities given by Eq. (3.1) below, and is impossible to calculate without knowledge of the choice-specific value functions.

In practice, "truncate" the infinite sum at some period T:

$$\tilde{V}(x, i = 1; \theta) = u(x, i = 1; \theta) + \beta \mathbb{E}_{x'|x,i=1} \mathbb{E}_{i'|x'} \mathbb{E}_{\epsilon''|i',x'} \left[u(x', i'; \theta) + \epsilon' \right.$$
$$+ \beta \mathbb{E}_{x''|x',i''} \mathbb{E}_{i''|x''} \mathbb{E}_{\epsilon'|i'',x''} \left[u(x'', i''; \theta) + \epsilon'' + \cdots \right.$$
$$+ \beta \mathbb{E}_{x^T|x^{T-1},i^{T-1}} \mathbb{E}_{i^T|x^T} \mathbb{E}_{\epsilon^T|i^T,x^T} \left[u(x^T, i^T; \theta) + \epsilon^T \right] \Big] \Big].$$

Also, the expectation $\mathbb{E}_{\epsilon|i,x}$ denotes the expectation of the ϵ_i conditional on choice i being taken, and current mileage x. For the logit case, there is a closed form:

$$\mathbb{E}[\epsilon_i|i, x] = \gamma - \log(Pr(i|x)),$$

where γ is Euler's constant (0.577...) and $Pr(i|x)$ is the choice probability of action i at state x.

Both of the other expectations in the above expressions are observed directly from the data.

Both choice-specific value functions can be simulated by (for $i = 1, 2$):

$$\tilde{V}(x, i; \theta) \approx = \frac{1}{S} \sum_s \left[u(x, i; \theta) + \beta \left[u(x'^s, i'^s; \theta) + \gamma - \log(\hat{P}(i'^s|x'^s)) \right. \right.$$
$$+ \beta \left[u(x''^s, i''^s; \theta) + \gamma - \log(\hat{P}(i''^s|x''^s)) + \beta \cdots \right] \Big] \Big],$$

where

- $x'^s \sim \hat{G}(\cdot|x, i)$,
- $i'^s \sim \hat{p}(\cdot|x'^s)$, $x''^s \sim \hat{G}(\cdot|x'^s, i'^s)$,
- etc.

In short, you simulate $\tilde{V}(x, i; \theta)$ by drawing S "sequences" of (i_t, x_t) with a initial value of (i, x), and computing the present-discounted utility correspond to each sequence. Then the simulation estimate of $\tilde{V}(x, i; \theta)$ is obtained as the sample average.

Given an estimate of $\tilde{V}(\cdot, i; \theta)$, you can get the *predicted choice probabilities*:

$$\tilde{p}(i = 1|x; \theta) \equiv \frac{\exp\left(\tilde{V}(x, i = 1; \theta)\right)}{\exp\left(\tilde{V}(x, i = 1; \theta)\right) + \exp\left(\tilde{V}(x, i = 0; \theta)\right)}, \quad (3.1)$$

and analogously for $\tilde{p}(i = 0|x; \theta)$. Note that the predicted choice probabilities are different from $\hat{p}(i|x)$, which are the actual choice probabilities computed from the actual data. The predicted choice probabilities depend on the parameters θ, whereas $\hat{p}(i|x)$ depend solely on the data.

3.1.2 Estimation: Match Hats to Tildes

One way to estimate θ is to minimize the distance between the predicted conditional choice probabilities, and the actual conditional choice probabilities:

$$\hat{\theta} = \text{argmin}_\theta || \hat{\mathbf{p}}(i = 1|x) - \tilde{\mathbf{p}}(i = 1|x; \theta) ||,$$

where $\mathbf{p}$ denotes a vector of probabilities, at various values of x.

Another way to estimate θ is very similar to the Berry/BLP method. We can calculate directly from the data.

$$\hat{\delta}_x \equiv \log \hat{p}(i = 1|x) - \log \hat{p}(i = 0|x).$$

Given the logit assumption, from Eq. (3.1), we know that,

$$\log \tilde{p}(i = 1|x) - \log \tilde{p}(i = 0|x) = \left[\tilde{V}(x, i = 1) - \tilde{V}(x, i = 0) \right].$$

Hence, by equating $\tilde{V}(x, i = 1) - \tilde{V}(x, i = 0)$ to $\hat{\delta}_x$, we obtain an alternative estimator for θ:

$$\bar{\theta} = \text{argmin}_\theta || \hat{\delta}_x - \left[\tilde{V}(x, i = 1; \theta) - \tilde{V}(x, i = 0; \theta) \right] ||.$$

3.1.3 A further shortcut in the discrete state case

In this section, for convenience, we will use Y instead of i to denote the action.

For the case when the state variables X are discrete, it turns out that, given knowledge of the CCP's $P(Y|X)$, solving for the value function is just equivalent to solving a system of linear equations. This was pointed out in Pesendorfer and Schmidt-Dengler (2008) and Aguirregabiria and Mira (2007). Specifically:

- Assume that choices Y and state variables X are all *discrete* (i.e., finite-valued). $|X|$ is cardinality of state space X. Here X includes just the observed state variables (not including the unobserved shocks ϵ).
- Per-period utilities:

$$u(Y, X, \epsilon_Y; \Theta) = \bar{u}(Y, X; \Theta) + \epsilon_Y,$$

where ϵ_Y, for $y = 1 \ldots Y$, are i.i.d. extreme value distributed with unit variance.

- Parameters Θ. The discount rate β is treated as known and fixed.
- Introduce some more specific notation. Define the integrated or *ex-ante* value function (before ϵ observed, and hence before the action Y is chosen)[4]:

$$W(X) = \mathbb{E}[V(X, \epsilon)|X].$$

Along the optimal dynamic path, at state X and optimal action Y, the continuation utility is,

$$\bar{u}(Y, X) + \epsilon_Y + \beta \sum_{X'} P(X'|X, Y) W(X').$$

This integrated value function satisfies a Bellman equation:

$$
\begin{aligned}
W(X) &= \sum_Y [P(Y|X) \{\bar{u}(Y, X) + \mathbb{E}(\epsilon_Y|Y, X)\}] \\
&\quad + \beta \sum_Y \sum_{X'} P(Y|X) P(X'|X, Y) W(X') \\
&= \sum_Y [P(Y|X) \{\bar{u}(Y, X) + \mathbb{E}(\epsilon_Y|Y, X)\}] \\
&\quad + \beta \sum_{X'} P(X'|X) W(X').
\end{aligned}
\tag{3.2}
$$

---

[4]Similar to Rust's $EV(\cdots)$ function, but *not the same*. See appendix.

- To derive the above, start with "real" Bellman equation:

$V(X, \epsilon)$

$$= \bar{u}(Y^*, X) + \sum_Y \epsilon_Y \mathbf{1}(Y = Y^*) + \beta \mathbb{E}_{X'|X,Y} \mathbb{E}_{\epsilon'|X'} V(X', \epsilon')$$

$$= \bar{u}(Y^*, X) + \sum_Y \epsilon_Y \mathbf{1}(Y = Y^*) + \beta \mathbb{E}_{X'|X,Y} W(X')$$

$\Rightarrow W(X)$

$$= \mathbb{E}_{\epsilon|X} V(X, \epsilon)$$

$$= \mathbb{E}_{Y^*,\epsilon|X} \left\{ \bar{u}(Y^*, X) + \sum_Y \epsilon_Y \mathbf{1}(Y = Y^*) + \beta \mathbb{E}_{X'|X,Y} W(X') \right\}$$

$$= \mathbb{E}_{Y^*|X} \mathbb{E}_{\epsilon|Y^*,X} \{\cdots\}$$

$$= \mathbb{E}_{Y^*|X} \left[\bar{u}(Y^*, X) + E[\epsilon_{Y^*}|Y^*, X] + \beta \mathbb{E}_{X'|X,Y} W(X') \right]$$

$$= \sum_Y P(Y = Y^*|X) [\cdots].$$

(*Note*: in the fourth line above, we first condition on the optimal choice Y^*, and take expectation of ϵ conditional on Y^*. The other way will not work.)

- In matrix notation, this is:

$$\bar{W}(\Theta) = \sum_{Y \in (0,1)} P(Y) * [\bar{u}(Y; \Theta) + \epsilon(Y)] + \beta \cdot F \cdot \bar{W}(\Theta)$$

$$\Leftrightarrow \bar{W}(\Theta) = (I - \beta F)^{-1} \left\{ \sum_{Y \in (0,1)} P(Y) * [\bar{u}(Y; \Theta) + \epsilon(Y)] \right\},$$

$$(3.3)$$

where

— $\bar{W}(\Theta)$ is the vector (each element denotes a different value of X) for the integrated value function at the parameter Θ;
— '*' denotes elementwise multiplication;
— F is the $|X|$-dimensional square matrix with (i,j)-element equal to $Pr(X' = j|X = i)$.

— $P(Y)$ is the $|X|$-vector consisting of elements $Pr(Y|X)$.
— $\bar{u}(Y)$ is the $|X|$-vector of per-period utilities $\bar{u}(Y;X)$.
— $\epsilon(Y)$ is an $|X|$-vector where each element is $E[\epsilon_Y|Y,X]$. For the logit assumptions, the closed-form is,

$$E[\epsilon_Y|Y,X] = \text{Euler's constant} - \log(P(Y|X)).$$

Euler's constant is 0.57721.

Based on this representation, P/SD propose a class of "least-squares" estimators, which are similar to HM-type estimators, except now we don't need to "forward-simulate" the value function. For instance:

- Let $\hat{P}(\bar{Y})$ denote the estimated vector of conditional choice probabilities, and $\hat{F}$ be the estimated transition matrix. Both of these can be estimated directly from the data.
- For each posited parameter value Θ, and given $(\hat{F}, \hat{P}(\bar{Y}))$ use Eq. (3.3) to evaluate the integrated value function $\bar{W}(X,\Theta)$, and derive the vector $\tilde{P}(\bar{Y};\Theta)$ of implied choice probabilities at Θ, which has elements

$$\tilde{P}(Y|X;\Theta) = \frac{\exp\left[\bar{u}(Y,X;\Theta) + \mathbb{E}_{X'|X,Y}W(X';\Theta)\right]}{\sum_Y \exp\left[\bar{u}(Y,X;\Theta) + \mathbb{E}_{X'|X,Y}W(X';\Theta)\right]}.$$

- Hence, Θ can be estimated as the parameter value minimizing the norm $||\hat{P}(\bar{Y}) - \tilde{P}(Y;\Theta)||$.

3.2   Semiparametric Identification of DDC Models

We can also use the Hotz–Miller estimation scheme as a basis for an argument regarding the identification of the underlying DDC model. In Markovian DDC models, without unobserved state variables, the Hotz–Miller routine exploits the fact that the Markov probabilities $x', d'|x, d$ are identified directly from the data, which can be factorized into

$$f(x', d'|x, d) = \underbrace{f(d'|x')}_{\text{CCP}} \cdot \underbrace{f(x'|x, d)}_{\text{state law of motion}} . \tag{3.4}$$

In this section, we argue that once these "reduced form" components of the model are identified, the remaining parts of the models — particularly, the per-period utility functions — can be identified without any further parametric assumptions. These arguments are drawn from Magnac and Thesmar (2002) and Bajari *et al.* (2007).

We make the following assumptions, which are standard in this literature:

1. Agents are optimizing in an infinite-horizon, stationary setting. Therefore, in the rest of this section, we use primes ''s to denote next-period values.
2. Actions D are chosen from the set $\mathcal{D} = \{0, 1, \ldots, K\}$.
3. The state variables are X.
4. The per-period utility from taking action $d \in \mathcal{D}$ in period t is:

$$u_d(X_t) + \epsilon_{d,t}, \ \forall d \in \mathcal{D}.$$

   The $\epsilon_{d,t}$'s are utility shocks which are independent of X_t, and distributed i.i.d with known distribution $F(\epsilon)$ across periods t and actions d. Let $\vec{\epsilon}_t \equiv (\epsilon_{0,1}, \epsilon_{1,t}, \ldots, \epsilon_{K,t})$.
5. From the data, the "conditional choice probabilities" CCPs

$$p_d(X) \equiv \text{Prob}(D = d|X),$$

   and the Markov transition kernel for X, denoted $p(X'|D, X)$, are identified.
6. $u_0(X)$, the per-period utility from $D = 0$, is normalized to zero, for all X.
7. β, the discount factor, is known.[5]

Following the arguments in Magnac and Thesmar (2002) and Bajari *et al.* (2007), we will show the nonparametric identification of $u_d(\cdot)$, $d = 1, \ldots, K$, the per-period utility functions for all actions except $D = 0$.

---

[5] Magnac and Thesmar (2002) discuss the possibility of identifying β via exclusion restrictions, but we do not pursue that here.

The Bellman equation for this dynamic optimization problem is,

$$V(X, \vec{\epsilon}) = \max_{d \in \mathcal{D}} \left(u_d(X) + \epsilon_d + \beta \mathbb{E}_{X', \vec{\epsilon}'|D,X} V(X', \vec{\epsilon}') \right),$$

where $V(X, \vec{\epsilon})$ denotes the value function. We define the choice-specific value function as,

$$V_d(X) \equiv u_d(X) + \beta \mathbb{E}_{X', \vec{\epsilon}'|D,X} V(X', \vec{\epsilon}').$$

Given these definitions, an agent's optimal choice when the state X is given by,

$$y^*(X) = \text{argmax}_{y \in \mathcal{D}} \left(V_d(X) + \epsilon_d \right).$$

Hotz and Miller (1993) and Magnac and Thesmar (2002) show that in this setting, there is a known one-to-one mapping, $q(X) : \mathbb{R}^K \to \mathbb{R}^K$, which maps the K-vector of choice probabilities $(p_1(X), \ldots, p_K(X))$ to the K-vector $(\Delta_1(X), \ldots, \Delta_K(X))$, where $\Delta_d(X)$ denotes the difference in choice-specific value functions

$$\Delta_d(X) \equiv V_d(X) - V_0(X).$$

Let the i-th element of $q(p_1(X), \ldots, p_K(X))$, denoted $q_i(X)$, be equal to $\Delta_i(X)$. The known mapping q derives just from $F(\epsilon)$, the known distribution of the utility shocks.

Hence, since the choice probabilities can be identified from the data, and the mapping q is known, the value function differences $\Delta_1(X), \ldots, \Delta_K(X)$ is also known.

Next, we note that the choice-specific value function also satisfies a Bellman-like equation:

$$V_d(X) = u_d(X) + \beta \mathbb{E}_{X'|X,D} \left[\mathbb{E}_{\vec{\epsilon}'} \max_{d' \in \mathcal{D}} (V_{d'}(X') + \epsilon'_{d'}) \right]$$

$$= u_d(X) + \beta \mathbb{E}_{X'|X,D} \left\{ V_0(X') + \left[\mathbb{E}_{\vec{\epsilon}'} \max_{d' \in \mathcal{D}} (\Delta_{d'}(X') + \epsilon'_{d'}) \right] \right\}$$

$$= u_d(X) + \beta \mathbb{E}_{X'|X,D} \left[H(\Delta_1(X'), \ldots, \Delta_K(X')) + V_0(X') \right],$$
$$(3.5)$$

where $H(\cdots)$ denotes McFadden's "social surplus" function, for random utility models (cf. Rust, 1994, pp. 3104ff). Like the q

mapping, H is a known function, which depends just on $F(\epsilon)$, the known distribution of the utility shocks.

Using the assumption that $u_0(X) = 0$, $\forall X$, the Bellman equation for $V_0(X)$ is

$$V_0(X) = \beta \mathbb{E}_{X'|X,D}\left[H(\Delta_1(X'), \dots, \Delta_K(X')) + V_0(X')\right]. \quad (3.6)$$

In this equation, everything is known (including, importantly, the distribution of $X'|X, D$), except the $V_0(\cdot)$ function. Hence, by iterating over Eq. (3.6), we can recover the $V_0(X)$ function. Once $V_0(\cdot)$ is known, the other choice-specific value functions can be recovered as

$$V_d(X) = \Delta_d(X) + V_0(X), \ \forall y \in \mathcal{D}, \ \forall X.$$

Finally, the per-period utility functions $u_d(X)$ can be recovered from the choice-specific value functions as

$$u_d(X) = V_d(X) - \beta \mathbb{E}_{X'|X,D}\left[H(\Delta_1(X'), \dots, \Delta_K(X')) + V_0(X')\right],$$

$$\forall y \in \mathcal{D}, \ \forall X,$$

where everything on the right-hand side is known.

Remark: For the case where $F(\epsilon)$ is the Type 1 Extreme Value distribution, the social surplus function is,

$$H(\Delta_1(X), \dots, \Delta_K(X)) = \log\left[1 + \sum_{d=1}^{K} \exp(\Delta_d(X))\right],$$

and the mapping q is such that:

$$q_d(X) = \Delta_d(X) = \log(p_d(X)) - \log(p_0(X)), \ \forall d = 1 \dots K,$$

where $p_0(X) \equiv 1 - \sum_{d=1}^{K} p_d(X)$.

Remark: The above argument also holds if ϵ_d is not independent of $\epsilon_{d'}$, and also if the joint distribution of $(\epsilon_0, \epsilon_1, \dots, \epsilon_K)$ is explicitly dependent on X. However, in that case, the mappings q_X and H_X will depend explicitly on X, and typically not be available in closed form, as in the multinomial logit (MNL) case. For this reason, practically all applications of this machinery maintain the MNL assumption.

3.3   Appendix: A Result for MNL Model

Show: for the MNL case, we have $E[\epsilon_j|\text{choice } j \text{ is chosen}] = \gamma - \log(P_j)$ where γ is Euler's constant $(0.577\ldots)$ and $Pr(d|x)$ is the choice probability of action j.

This closed-form expression has been used much in the literature on estimating dynamic models: e.g., Eq. (12) in Aguirregabiria and Mira (2007) or Eq. (2.22) in Hotz *et al.* (1994).

Use the fact: for a univariate extreme value variate with parameter a, CDF $F(\epsilon) = \exp(-ae^{-\epsilon})$, and density $f(\epsilon) = \exp(-ae^{-\epsilon})(ae^{-\epsilon})$, we have

$$E(\epsilon) = \log a + \gamma, \quad \gamma = 0.577.$$

Also use McFadden's (1978) results for generalized extreme value distribution:

- For a function $G(e^{V_0}, \ldots, e^{V_J})$, we define the generalized extreme value distribution of $(\epsilon_0, \ldots, \epsilon_j)$ with joint CDF $F(\epsilon_0, \ldots, \epsilon_J) = \exp\{-G(e^{\epsilon_0}, \ldots, e^{\epsilon_J})\}$.
- $G(\ldots)$ is a homogeneous-degree-1 function, with nonnegative odd partial derivatives and nonpositive even partial derivatives.
- **Theorem 1.** For a random utility model where agent chooses according to $j = \text{argmax}_{j' \in \{0,1,\ldots,J\}} U_j = V_j + \epsilon_j$, the choice probabilities are given by

$$P(j) = \int_{-\infty}^{\infty} F_j(V_j + \epsilon_j - V_0, V_j + \epsilon_j - V_1, \ldots, V_j + \epsilon_j - V_J)d\epsilon_j$$

$$= \frac{e^{V_j}G_j(e^{V_0}, \ldots, e^{V_J})}{G(e^{V_0}, \ldots, e^{V_J})}.$$

- **Corollary.** Total expected surplus is given by,

$$\bar{U} = \mathbb{E}\max_{j}(V_j + \epsilon_j) = \gamma + \log(G(e^{V_0}, \ldots, e^{V_J})),$$

and choice probabilities by $P_j = \frac{\partial \bar{U}}{\partial V_j}$. For this reason, $G(\ldots)$ is called the "social surplus function".

In what follows, we use McFadden's shorthand of $\langle V_{j'} \rangle$ to denote a $J+1$ vector with $j'-th$ component equal to $V_{j'-1}$ for $j' = 1, \ldots, J$.

Imitating the proof for the corollary above, we can derive that (defining $a = G(\langle e^{V_{j'}} \rangle)$)

$$\mathbb{E}(V_j + \epsilon_j | j \text{ is chosen})$$

$$= \frac{1}{P_j} \int_{-\infty}^{+\infty} (V_j + \epsilon_j) F_j(\langle V_j + \epsilon_j - V_{j'} \rangle) d\epsilon_j$$

$$= \frac{1}{P_j} \int_{-\infty}^{+\infty} (V_j + \epsilon_j) \exp(-G(\langle e^{-V_j - \epsilon_j + V_{j'}} \rangle))$$

$$\times G_j(\langle e^{-V_j - \epsilon_j + V_{j'}} \rangle) e^{-\epsilon_j} d\epsilon_j$$

$$= \frac{a}{e^{V_j} G_j(\langle e^{V_{j'}} \rangle)} \int_{-\infty}^{+\infty} (V_j + \epsilon_j) \exp(-ae^{-V_j - \epsilon_j})$$

$$\times G_j(\langle e^{V_{j'}} \rangle) e^{-\epsilon_j} d\epsilon_j \qquad \text{(by props. of } G\text{)}$$

$$= \int_{-\infty}^{+\infty} (V_j + \epsilon_j) \exp(-ae^{V_j - \epsilon_j}) ae^{-V_j} e^{-\epsilon_j} d\epsilon_j$$

$$= \int_{-\infty}^{+\infty} w \exp(-ae^{-w}) ae^w dw \qquad (V_j + \epsilon_j \to w)$$

$$= \log(a) + \gamma.$$

For the MNL model, we have $G(\langle e^{V_{j'}} \rangle) = \sum_{j'} e^{V_{j'}}$. For this case $P_j = \exp(V_j)/G(\langle e^{V_{j'}} \rangle)$, and $G_j(\cdots) = 1$ for all j. Then

$$\mathbb{E}[\epsilon_j | j \text{ is chosen}] = \log(a) + \gamma - (V_j - V_0) - V_0$$

$$= \log(G(\langle e^{V_{j'}} \rangle)) + \gamma - \log(P_j)$$

$$+ \log(P_0) - V_0 \quad (\text{using } V_j - V_0 = \log(P_j/P_0))$$

$$= \log(G(\langle e^{V_{j'}} \rangle)) + \gamma - \log(P_j) + V_0$$
$$- \log(G(\langle e^{V_{j'}} \rangle)) - V_0$$
$$= \gamma - \log(P_j).$$

3.4 Appendix: Relations Between Different Value Function Notions

Here we delve into the differences between the "real" value function $V(x, \epsilon)$, the $EV(x, y)$ function from Rust (1994), and the integrated or *ex-ante* value function $W(x)$ from Aguirregabiria and Mira (2007) and Pesendorfer and Schmidt-Dengler (2008).

By definition, Rust's EV function is defined as:

$$EV(x, y) = \mathbb{E}_{x', \epsilon'|x, y} V(x', \epsilon').$$

By definition, the integrated value function is defined as

$$W(x) = \mathbb{E}[V(X, \epsilon)|X = x].$$

By iterated expectations,

$$EV(x, y) = \mathbb{E}_{x', \epsilon'|x, y} V(x', \epsilon')$$
$$= \mathbb{E}_{x'|x, y} \mathbb{E}_{\epsilon'|x'} V(x', \epsilon')$$
$$= \mathbb{E}_{x'|x, y} W(x'),$$

given the relationship between the EV and integrated value functions.

Hence, the "choice-specific value function" (without the ϵ) is defined as:

$$\bar{v}(x, y) \equiv u(x, y) + \beta \mathbb{E}_{x', \epsilon'|x, y} V(x', \epsilon')$$
$$= u(x, y) + \beta EV(x, y)$$
$$= u(x, y) + \beta \mathbb{E}_{x'|x, y} W(x').$$

Also note

$$V(x, \epsilon) = \max_y \{\bar{v}(x, y) + \epsilon_y\}$$

$$\Rightarrow W(x) = \mathbb{E}\left[\max_y \{\bar{v}(x, y) + \epsilon_y\} | x\right]$$

which corresponds to the *social surplus function* of this DDC model.

Bibliography

Aguirregabiria, V. and P. Mira (2007): "Sequential Estimation of Dynamic Discrete Games," *Econometrica*, **75**, 1–53.

Bajari, P., V. Chernozhukov, H. Hong and D. Nekipelov (2007): "Nonparametric and Semiparametric Analysis of a Dynamic Game Model," Manuscript, University of Minnesota.

Hotz, J. and R. Miller (1993): "Conditional Choice Probabilties and the Estimation of Dynamic Models," *Rev. Econ. Stud.*, **60**, 497–529.

Hotz, J., R. Miller, S. Sanders and J. Smith (1994): "A Simulation Estimator for Dynamic Models of Discrete Choice," *Rev. Econ. Stud.*, **61**, 265–289.

Magnac, T. and D. Thesmar (2002): "Identifying Dynamic Discrete Decision Processes," *Econometrica*, **70**, 801–816.

McFadden, D. (1978): "Modelling the Choice of Residential Location," in *Spatial Interaction Theory and Residential Location*, eds. by A. K. *et al.* North-Holland.

Pesendorfer, M. and P. Schmidt-Dengler (2008): "Asymptotic Least Squares Estimators for Dynamic Games," *Rev. Econ. Stud.*, **75**, 901–928.

Rust, J. (1994): "Structural Estimation of Markov Decision Processes," in *Handbook of Econometrics*, eds. R. Engle and D. McFadden, Vol. 4, pp. 3082–146. North Holland.

Chapter 4

Single-agent Dynamic Models: Part 3

4.1 Model with Persistence in Unobservables ("Unobserved State Variables")

Up to now, we have considered models satisfying Rust's "conditional independence" assumption on the ϵ's. This rules out persistence in unobservables, which can be economically meaningful.

4.1.1 Example: Pakes (1986) patent renewal model

Pakes (1986). How much are patents worth? This question is important because it *inform* public policy as to optimal patent length and design. Are patents a sufficient means of rewarding innovation?

- Q_A: value of patent at age A;
- Goal of paper is to estimate Q_A using data on their renewal. Q_A is inferred from patent renewal process via a *structural model* of optimal patent renewal behavior;
- Treat patent renewal system as exogenous (only in Europe);

- For $a = 1, \ldots, L$, a patent can be renewed by paying the fee c_a;
- Timing:
  - At age $a = 1$, patent holder obtains period revenue r_1 from patent.
  - Decides whether or not to renew. If renewed, then pay c_1, and proceed to age $a = 2$.
  - At age $a = 2$, patent holder obtains period revenue r_2 from patent.
  - Decides whether or not to renew. If renewed, then pay c_2, and proceed to age $a = 3$. And so on...
- Let V_a denote the value of patent at age a.

$$V_a \equiv \max_{t \in [a,L]} \sum_{a'=1}^{L-a} \beta^{a'} R(a + a'), \text{ where}$$

$$R(a) = \begin{cases} r_a - c_a & \text{if } t \geq a \text{ (when you hold onto patent)}, \\ 0 & \text{if } t < a \text{ (after you allow patent to expire)}, \end{cases}$$
$$(4.1)$$

where t denotes the age at which the agent allows the patent to expire, and is the agent's choice variable in this problem. This type of problem is called an "optimal stopping" problem. $R(a)$ denotes the profits from the patent during the ath year. The sequence $R(1), R(2), \ldots$ is a "controlled" stochastic process: it is inherently random, but is also affected by agent's actions.

- Since the maximal age L is finite, this is a finite-horizon (nonstationary) dynamic optimization problem.
- The state variable of this DO problem is r_a, the single-period revenue.
- Finite-horizon DO problems are solved via *backward recursion*. The value functions $\{V_1(\cdot), V_2(\cdot), \ldots, V_a(\cdot), \ldots, V_L(\cdot)\}$

are recursively related via Bellman's equation:

$$V_a(r_a) = \max \left\{ 0, \ \underbrace{r_a + \beta E\left[V_{a+1}(r_{a+1})|\Omega_a\right] - c_a}_{\equiv Q_a \text{ value of age } a \text{ patent}} \right\}.$$

RHS means you will choose to renew the patent if $Q_a - c_a > 0$.
Ω_a: history up to age a, $= \{r_1, r_2, \ldots, r_a\}$.
Expectation is over $r_{a+1}|\Omega_a$. The sequence of conditional distributions $G_a \equiv F(r_{a+1}|\Omega_a)$, $a = 1, 2, \ldots$, is an important component of the model specification. Pakes' assumptions are as follows:

$$r_{a+1} = \begin{cases} 0 & \text{with prob. } \exp(-\theta r_a), \\ \max(\delta r_a, z) & \text{with prob. } 1 - \exp(-\theta r_a), \end{cases} \quad (4.2)$$

where density of z is $q_a = \frac{1}{\sigma_a} \exp\left[-(\gamma + z)/\sigma_a\right]$ and $\sigma_a = \phi^{a-1}\sigma$, $a = 1, \ldots, L-1$.
δ, θ, γ, ϕ, and σ are the important structural parameters of the model.

- So break down maximization problem into period-by-period problem, where each period agent decides whether or not to incur cost c_a and gain the value of the patent $Q_a = r_a +$ "option value." Option value captures the value in keeping patent alive in order to make a choice tomorrow.

   Implications of model seen graphically:

- Drop out at age a if $c_a > Q_a$.
- Optimal decision characterized by "cutoff points":

$$Q_a > c_a \Leftrightarrow r_a > \bar{r}_a.$$

This feature is due to Assumption A3.3, which ensures that Q_a is increasing in r_a (so that Q_a and c_a only cross once)

- The sequence of cutoff points $\bar{r}_a < \bar{r}_{a+1} < \cdots < \bar{r}_{L-1}$: ensured by Assumption A3.4.

4.1.2 Estimation: Likelihood function and simulation

In this section, we consider estimation of the Pakes patent renewal model. For ease of comparison with the Rust model from before, we use ϵ to denote the unobserved state variable, which in the Pakes model corresponds to the patent revenue r_t. Furthermore, we use i_t to denote the choice (control) variable; it is equal to zero if patent is renewed, and equal to one if patent expires.

Consider one patent. Let $\tilde{T}$ denote the age at which the patent is allowed to expire. Due to the setup of the problem, $\tilde{T} \leq L$, the maximal age of the patent. Let $T = \min(L-1, \tilde{T})$ denote the number of periods in which the agent makes an active patent renewal decision. We model the agent's decisions in periods $t = 1, \ldots, T$.

ϵ evolves as a first-order Markov process, evolving according to: $F(\epsilon'|\epsilon)$. We denote the (age-specific) policy function by $i_t^*(\epsilon)$.

Now the likelihood function for this patent is:

$$l\left(i_t, \ldots, i_T | \epsilon_0, i_0; \theta\right) = \prod_{t=1}^{T} \text{Prob}\left(i_t | i_0, \ldots, i_{t-1}; \epsilon_0, \theta\right). \qquad (4.3)$$

Note that because of the serially correlated ϵ's, there is still dependence between (say) i_t and i_{t-2}, even after conditioning on (i_{t-1}): compare the likelihood function in the Rust lecture notes and Eq. (4.3). In other words, the *joint process* $\{i_t, \epsilon_t\}$ is first-order Markov, but the *marginal* process $\{i_t\}$ is not first-order Markov. Also, because of serial correlation in the ϵ's, the $\text{Prob}\left(i_t | i_0, \ldots, i_{t-1}; \theta\right)$ no longer has a closed form. Thus, we consider simulating the likelihood function.

Note that simulation is part of the "outer loop" of nested fixed point estimation routine. So at the point when we simulate, we already know the policy functions $i_t^*(\epsilon; \theta)$. (How would you compute this?)

4.1.3   "Crude" frequency simulator: Naive approach

In this section, we describe a naive approach to simulating the likelihood of this model. *This is not something we want to do in practice, but we describe it here in order to contrast it with the particle-filtering (importance sampling) approach, which we describe in the next section.*

For simulation purposes, it is most convenient to go back to the full likelihood function (the first line of Eq. (4.3)):

$$l(i_1, \ldots, i_T | i_0, \epsilon_0; \theta).$$

Note that because the ϵ's are serially correlated, we also need to condition on an initial value ϵ_0 (which, for simplicity, we assume to be known). Pakes does something slightly more complicated — he assumes that the *distribution* of ϵ_0 is known.

Because i is discrete, the likelihood is the joint probability,

$$\Pr(i_t^*(\epsilon_t; \theta) = i_t, \ \forall t = 1, \ldots, T),$$

where the i_t's denote the observed sequence of choices. The probability is taken over by the distribution of $(\epsilon_1, \ldots, \epsilon_T | \epsilon_0)$.

Let $F(\epsilon_{t+1} | \epsilon_t; \theta)$. Then the above probability can be expressed as the integral:

$$\int \cdots \int \prod_t \mathbf{1}(i_t^*(\epsilon_t; \theta) = i_t) \prod_t dF(\epsilon_t | \epsilon_{t-1}; \theta).$$

We can simulate this integral by drawing sequences of (ϵ_t). For each simulation draw $s = 1, \ldots, S$, we take as initial values

i_0, ϵ_0. Then:

- Generate $\left(\epsilon_1^s, i_1^s\right)$:
    1. Generate $\epsilon_1^s \sim F(\epsilon_1|\epsilon_0)$.
    2. Compute $i_1^s = i_1^*\left(\epsilon_1^s; \theta\right)$.
- Generate $\left(\epsilon_2^s, i_2^s\right)$:
    1. Generate $\epsilon_2^s \sim F\left(\epsilon_2|\epsilon_1^s\right)$.
    2. Subsequently compute $i_2^s = i_2^*\left(\epsilon_2^s; \theta\right)$

... and so on, up to (ϵ_T^s, i_T^s).

Then, for the case where (i, x) are both discrete (which is the case in Rust's paper), we can approximate

$$l\left(i_t, \ldots, i_T | \epsilon_0, i_0; \theta\right) \approx \frac{1}{S} \sum_s \prod_{t=1}^T \mathbf{1}\left(i_t^s = i_t\right).$$

That is, the simulated likelihood is the frequency of the simulated sequences which match the observed sequence.

This is a "crude" frequency simulator. Clearly, if T is long, or S is modest, the simulated likelihood is likely to be zero. What is commonly done in practice is to smooth the indicator functions in this simulated likelihood.

4.1.4 Importance sampling approach: Particle filtering

Another approach is to employ importance sampling in simulating the likelihood function. This is not straightforward, given the across-time dependence between (i_t, ϵ_t). Here, we consider a new simulation approach, called *particle filtering*. It is a recursive approach to simulate dependent sequences of random variables. The presentation here draws from Fernandez-Villaverde and Rubio-Ramirez (2007) (see also Flury and Shephard, 2008). This is also called "non-Gaussian Kalman filtering."

We need to introduce some notation, and be more specific about features of the model. Let:

- $y_t \equiv \{i_t\}$. $y^t \equiv \{y_t, \dots, y_t\}$. These are the *observed sequences* in the data.
- Evolution of utility shocks: $\epsilon_t | \epsilon_{t-1} \sim f(\epsilon' | \epsilon)$ (Ignore dependence of distribution of ϵ on age t for convenience).
- As before, the policy function is $i_t = i^*(\epsilon_t)$.
- Let $\epsilon^t \equiv \{\epsilon_1, \dots, \epsilon_t\}$.
- The initial values y_0 and ϵ_0 are known.

Go back to the factorized likelihood:

$$l(y^T | y_0, \epsilon_0) = \prod_{t=1}^{T} l(y_t | y^{t-1}, y_0, \epsilon_0)$$

$$= \prod_{t} \int l(y_t | \epsilon^t, y^{t-1}) p(\epsilon^t | y^{t-1}) d\epsilon^t$$

$$\approx \prod_{t} \frac{1}{S} \sum_{s} l(y_t | \epsilon^{t|t-1,s}, y^{t-1}), \qquad (4.4)$$

where in the second to last line, we omit conditioning on (y_0, ϵ_0) for convenience. In the last line, $\epsilon^{t|t-1,s}$ denotes simulated draws of ϵ^t from $p(\epsilon^t | y^{t-1})$.

Consider the two terms in the second to last line:

- The first term $l(y_t | \epsilon^t, y^{t-1})$:

$$l(y_t | \epsilon^t, y^{t-1}) = p(i_t | \epsilon^t, y^{t-1})$$

$$= p(i_t | \epsilon_t) = \mathbf{1}(i(\epsilon_t) = i_t). \qquad (4.5)$$

Clearly, this term can be explicitly calculated, for a given value of ϵ_t.

- The second term $p(\epsilon^t | y^{t-1})$ is, generally, not obtainable in closed form. So numerical integration is not feasible. The particle filtering algorithm permits us to draw sequences of ϵ^t from $p(\epsilon^t|y^{t-1})$, for every period t. Hence, the second-to-last line of Eq. (4.4) can be approximated by simulation, as shown in the last line.

Particle filtering proposes a recursive approach to draw sequences from $p(\epsilon^t|y^{t-1})$, for every t. Easiest way to proceed is just to describe the algorithm.

First period, $t = 1$: In order to simulate the integral corresponding to the first period, we need to draw from $p(\epsilon^1|y^0,\epsilon_0)$. This is easy. We draw $\{\epsilon^{1|0,s}\}_{s=1}^S$, according to $f(\epsilon'|\epsilon_0)$. The notation $\epsilon^{1|0,s}$ makes explicitly that the ϵ is a draw from $p(\epsilon^1|y^0,\epsilon_0)$. Using these S draws, we can evaluate the simulated likelihood for period 1, in Eq. (4.4). We are done for period $t = 1$.

Second period, $t = 2$: We need to draw from $p(\epsilon^2|y^1)$. Factorize this as:

$$p(\epsilon^2|y^1) = p(\epsilon^1|y^1) \cdot p(\epsilon_2|\epsilon^1). \qquad (4.6)$$

Recall our notation that $\epsilon^2 \equiv \{\epsilon_1, \epsilon_2\}$. Consider simulating from each term separately:

- Getting a draw from $p(\epsilon^1|y^1)$, given that we already have draws $\{\epsilon^{1|0,s}\}$ from $p(\epsilon^1|y_0)$, from the previous period $t = 1$, is the heart of particle filtering.

  We use the principle of importance sampling: by Bayes' Rule,

$$p(\epsilon^1|y^1) \propto p(y_1|\epsilon^1, y^0) \cdot p(\epsilon^1|y^0). \qquad (4.7)$$

Hence, if our desired sampling density is $p(\epsilon^1|y^1)$, but we actually have draws $\{\epsilon^{1|0,s}\}$ from $p(\epsilon^1|y^0)$, then the importance sampling weight for the draw $\epsilon^{1|0,s}$ is proportional to,

$$\tau_1^s \equiv p(y_1|\epsilon^{1|0,s}, y^0).$$

Note that this coincides with the likelihood contribution for period 1, evaluated at the shock $\epsilon^{1|0,s}$.

The SIR (Sampling/Importance Resampling) algorithm in Rubin (1988) proposes that, making S draws with replacement from the samples $\{\epsilon^{1|0,s}\}_{s=1}^{S}$, using weights proportional to τ_1^s, yields draws from the desired density $p(\epsilon^1|y^1)$, which we denote $\{\epsilon^{1,s}\}_{s=1}^{S}$. This is the **filtering** step.

- For the second term in Eq. (4.6): we simply draw one ϵ_2^s from $f(\epsilon'|\epsilon^{1,s})$, for each draw $\epsilon^{1,s}$ from the filtering step. This is the **prediction** step.

By combining the draws from these two terms, we have $\{\epsilon^{2|1,s}\}_{s=1}^{S}$, which is S drawn sequences from $p(\epsilon^2|y^1)$. Using these S draws, we can evaluate the simulated likelihood for period 2, in Eq. (4.4).

Third period, $t = 3$: start again by factoring

$$p(\epsilon^3|y^2) = p(\epsilon^2|y^2) \cdot p(\epsilon_3|\epsilon^2). \tag{4.8}$$

As above, drawing from the first term requires filtering the draws $\{\epsilon^{2|1,s}\}_{s=1}^{S}$, from the previous period $t = 2$, to obtain draws $\{\epsilon^{2,s}\}_{s=1}^{S}$. Given these draws, draw $\epsilon_3^s \sim f(\epsilon'|\epsilon^{2,s})$ for each s.

And so on. By the last period $t = T$, you have,

$$\left\{ \{\epsilon^{t|t-1,s}\}_{s=1}^{S} \right\}_{t=1}^{T}.$$

Hence, the factorized likelihood in Eq. (4.4) can be approximated by simulation as

$$\prod_t \frac{1}{S} \sum_s l(y_t|\epsilon^{t|t-1,s}, y^{t-1}).$$

As noted above, the likelihood term $l(y_t|\epsilon^{t|t-1,s}, y^{t-1})$ coincides with the simulation weight τ_t^s. Hence, the simulated likelihood can also be constructed as

$$\log l(y^T|y_0,\epsilon_0) = \sum_t \log \left\{ \frac{1}{S}\sum_s \tau_t^s \right\}.$$

Summary of particle filter simulator:

1. Start by drawing $\{\epsilon^{1|0,s}\}_{s=1}^S$ from $p(\epsilon^1|y^0,\epsilon_0)$.
2. In period t, we start with $\{\epsilon^{t-1|t-2,s}\}_{s=1}^S$, draws from $p(\epsilon^{t-1}|y^{t-2},\epsilon_0)$.
   (a) **Filter step:** Calculate proportion weights $\tau_{t-1}^s \equiv p(y_{t-1}|\epsilon^{t-1|t-2,s},y^{t-2})$ using Eq. (4.5). Draw $\{\epsilon^{t-1|t-1,s}\}_{s=1}^S$ by resampling from $\{\epsilon^{t-1|t-2,s}\}_{s=1}^S$ with weights τ_{t-1}^s.
   (b) **Prediction step:** Draw ϵ_t^s from $p(\epsilon_t|\epsilon^{t-1|t-1,s})$, for $s = 1,\ldots,S$. Combine to get $\{\epsilon^{t|t-1,s}\}_{s=1}^S$.
3. Set $t = t + 1$, and go back to step 2. Stop when $t = T + 1$.

Note the difference between this recursive simulator, and the crude simulator described previously. The crude simulator draws S sequences, and essentially assigns zero weight to all sequences which do not match the observed sequence in the data. In contrast, in particle filtering, in each period t, we just keep sequences where predicted choices match observed choice *that period*. This will lead to more accurate evaluation of the likelihood. Note that S should be large enough (relative to the sequence length T) so that the filtering step does not end up assigning almost all weight to one particular sequence $\epsilon^{t|t-1,s}$ in any period t.

4.1.5 Nonparametric identification of Markovian Dynamic Discrete Choice (DDC) models with unobserved state variables

In this section, we consider nonparametric identification in **Markov dynamic choice models** with *serially correlated* *unobserved state variables.* We summarize the main findings from Hu and Shum (2008). Consider the fundamental "data problem":

- Model follows first-order Markov process $\{W_t, X_t^*\}_{t=1}^T$
- But only $\{W_t\}$ for $t = 1, 2, \ldots, T$ is observed,

  — In many empirical dynamic models, $W_t = (Y_t, M_t)$:

    * Y_t is choice variable: agent's action in period t.
    * M_t is observed state variable.

  — X_t^* is persistent (serially-correlated) unobserved state variable.

- Focus on nonparametric identification of Markov law of motion $\Pr(W_t, X_t^* | W_{t-1}, X_{t-1}^*)$.
  For estimation of models: structural components fully summarized by this law of motion.
- New features of our results (relative to literature):

  — X_t^* serially correlated: *unobserved state variable.*
  — X_t^* can be continuous or discrete.
  — Feedback: evolution of X_t^* can depend on W_{t-1}, X_{t-1}^*.
  — Novel identification approach: use recent findings from nonclassical measurement error econometrics: Hu (2008), Hu and Schennach (2008) and Carroll, Chen, and Hu (2009).

Basic setup: conditions for identification

- Consider dynamic processes $\{(W_T, X_T^*), \ldots, (W_t, X_t^*), \ldots, (W_1, X_1^*)\}_i$, identically independently distributed (i.i.d.) across agents $i \in \{1, 2, \ldots, n\}$.
- The researcher has panel data: $\{W_{t+1}, W_t, W_{t-1}, W_{t-2}, W_{t-3}\}_i$ for many agents i (5 obs).
- Assumption: (Dimension-reduction) The process (W_t, X_t^*) satisfies,

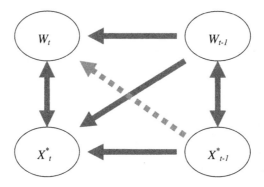

Figure 4.1:   Flowchart for Assumption (Dimension = Reduction).

(i) *First-order Markov:*

$$f_{W_t, X_t^* | W_{t-1}, \ldots, W_1, X_{t-1}^*, \ldots, X_1^*} = f_{W_t, X_t^* | W_{t-1}, X_{t-1}^*}$$

— Standard in most applications of DDC models.

(ii) *Limited feedback* (Figure 4.1):

$$f_{W_t | W_{t-1}, X_t^*, X_{t-1}^*} = f_{W_t | W_{t-1}, X_t^*}.$$

— Satisfied in many empirical applications.
— think of as timing restriction (X_t^* occurs before M_t).

Identification argument: discrete case

- Build intuition by considering discrete case:

$$\forall t, \ X_t^* \in \mathcal{X}^* \equiv \{1, 2, \ldots, J\}.$$

- For convenience, assume W_t also discrete, with same support $\mathcal{W}_t = \mathcal{X}_t^*$.
- In what follows:

   — "L" denotes J-square matrix.
   — "D" denotes J-diagonal matrix.

- Define the J-by-J matrices (fix w_t and w_{t-1}),

$$L_{W_{t+1},w_t|w_{t-1},W_{t-2}} = \left[f_{W_{t+1},W_t|W_{t-1},W_{t-2}}(i, w_t|w_{t-1}, j) \right]_{i,j}$$

$$L_{W_{t+1}|w_t,X_t^*} = \left[f_{W_{t+1}|W_t,X_t^*}(i|w_t, j) \right]_{i,j}$$

$$L_{X_t^*|w_{t-1},W_{t-2}} = \left[f_{X_t^*|W_{t-1},W_{t-2}}(i|w_{t-1}, j) \right]_{i,j}$$

$$D_{w_t|w_{t-1},X_t^*}$$
$$= \begin{bmatrix} f_{W_t|W_{t-1},X_t^*}(w_t|w_{t-1}, 1) & 0 & 0 \\ 0 & \cdots & 0 \\ 0 & 0 & f_{W_t|W_{t-1},X_t^*}(w_t|w_{t-1}, J) \end{bmatrix}.$$

- $\boxed{}$: elements identified from data.
- : elements identified in proof.

For fixed (w_t, w_{t-1}), in matrix notation: **Lemma 2. representation of** $f_{W_t,X_t^*|W_{t-1},X_{t-1}^*}$: The Markovian law of motion

$$L_{w_t,X_t^*|w_{t-1},X_{t-1}^*}$$
$$= L_{W_{t+1}|w_t,X_t^*}^{-1} \boxed{L_{W_{t+1},w_t|w_{t-1},W_{t-2}} L_{W_t|w_{t-1},W_{t-2}}^{-1}} L_{W_t|w_{t-1},X_{t-1}^*}.$$

Proof of Lemma 2.

- Main equation: for any (w_t, w_{t-1}),

$$\boxed{L_{W_{t+1},w_t|w_{t-1},W_{t-2}}}$$
$$= L_{W_{t+1}|w_t,X^*} \, L_{w_t,X_t^*|w_{t-1},W_{t-2}}$$
$$= L_{W_{t+1}|w_t,X^*} \, L_{w_t,X_t^*|w_{t-1},X_{t-1}^*} L_{X_{t-1}^*|w_{t-1},W_{t-2}}.$$

- Similarly: $\boxed{L_{W_t|w_{t-1},W_{t-2}}} = L_{W_t|w_{t-1},X_{t-1}^*} L_{X_{t-1}^*|w_{t-1},W_{t-2}}.$

- Manipulating above two equations: $L_{w_t,X_t^*|w_{t-1},X_{t-1}^*}$,

$$= L_{W_{t+1}|w_t,X^*}^{-1} \boxed{L_{W_{t+1},w_t|w_{t-1},W_{t-2}}} L_{X_{t-1}^*|w_{t-1},W_{t-2}}^{-1}$$

$$= L_{W_{t+1}|w_t,X_t^*}^{-1} \boxed{L_{W_{t+1},w_t|w_{t-1},W_{t-2}}} L_{W_t|w_{t-1},W_{t-2}}^{-1} L_{W_t|w_{t-1},X_{t-1}^*}.$$

- Hence, all we must identify are $L_{W_{t+1}|w_t,X_t^*}$ and $L_{W_t|w_{t-1},X_{t-1}^*}$.

Lemma 3. From $\boxed{f_{W_{t+1},w_t|w_{t-1},W_{t-2}}}$, identify $\underline{L_{W_{t+1}|w_t,X_t^*}}$.
  Lemma 3 implies:

- Stationary case: $L_{W_{t+1}|w_t,X_t^*} = L_{W_t|w_{t-1},X_{t-1}^*}$, so Lemma 3 implies identification (4 obs).
- Nonstationary case: apply Lemma 3 in turn to $\boxed{f_{W_{t+1},w_t|w_{t-1},W_{t-2}}}$ and $\boxed{f_{W_t,w_{t-1}|w_{t-2},W_{t-3}}}$ (5 obs).

Proof of Lemma 3.

- Similar to Carroll, Chen, and Hu (2008)
- Key factorization: $\boxed{f_{W_{t+1},W_t,W_{t-1},W_{t-2}}}$

$$= \iint f_{W_{t+1},W_t,W_{t-1},W_{t-2},X_t^*,X_{t-1}^*} \, dx_t^* dx_{t-1}^*$$

$$= \iint f_{W_{t+1}|W_t,X_t^*} \cdot f_{W_t,X_t^*|W_{t-1},X_{t-1}^*}$$
$$\cdot f_{W_{t-1},W_{t-2},X_{t-1}^*} \, dx_t^* dx_{t-1}^*$$

$$= \iint f_{W_{t+1}|W_t,X_t^*} \cdot f_{W_t|W_{t-1},X_t^*,X_{t-1}^*}$$
$$\cdot f_{X_t^*,X_{t-1}^*,W_{t-1},W_{t-2}} \, dx_t^* dx_{t-1}^*$$

$$= \int f_{W_{t+1}|W_t,X_t^*} f_{W_t|W_{t-1},X_t^*} \cdot f_{X_t^*,W_{t-1},W_{t-2}} \, dx_t^*.$$

- Discrete-case, matrix notation (for any fixed w_t, w_{t-1}) matrix-main details:

$$\boxed{L_{W_{t+1},w_t|w_{t-1},W_{t-2}}} = L_{W_{t+1}|w_t,X_t^*} D_{w_t|w_{t-1},X_t^*} L_{X_t^*|w_{t-1},W_{t-2}}.$$

- Important feature: for (w_t, w_{t-1}),

$$\boxed{L_{W_{t+1}, w_t | w_{t-1}, W_{t-2}}} = \underbrace{L_{W_{t+1} | w_t, X_t^*}}_{\text{no } w_{t-1}} \underbrace{D_{w_t | w_{t-1}, X_t^*}}_{\text{only } J \text{ unkwns.}} \underbrace{L_{X_t^* | w_{t-1}, W_{t-2}}}_{\text{no } w_t} \cdot$$

- For (w_t, w_{t-1}), $(\overline{w}_t, w_{t-1})$, $(\overline{w}_t, \overline{w}_{t-1})$ $(w_t, \overline{w}_{t-1})$,

$$\boxed{L_{W_{t+1}, w_t | w_{t-1}, W_{t-2}}} = L_{W_{t+1} | w_t, X_t^*} D_{w_t | w_{t-1}, X_t^*} \overbrace{L_{X_t^* | w_{t-1}, W_{t-2}}},$$

$$\boxed{L_{W_{t+1}, \overline{w}_t | w_{t-1}, W_{t-2}}} = \overbrace{L_{W_{t+1} | \overline{w}_t, X_t^*}} D_{\overline{w}_t | w_{t-1}, X_t^*} \overbrace{L_{X_t^* | w_{t-1}, W_{t-2}}},$$

$$\boxed{L_{W_{t+1}, \overline{w}_t | \overline{w}_{t-1}, W_{t-2}}} = \overbrace{L_{W_{t+1} | \overline{w}_t, X_t^*}} D_{\overline{w}_t | \overline{w}_{t-1}, X_t^*} \overbrace{L_{X_t^* | \overline{w}_{t-1}, W_{t-2}}},$$

$$\boxed{L_{W_{t+1}, w_t | \overline{w}_{t-1}, W_{t-2}}} = L_{W_{t+1} | w_t, X_t^*} D_{w_t | \overline{w}_{t-1}, X_t^*} \overbrace{L_{X_t^* | \overline{w}_{t-1}, W_{t-2}}} \cdot$$

- Assume: (Invertibility) LHS invertible, which is testable.
- Eliminate $L_{X_t^* | w_{t-1}, W_{t-2}}$ using first two equations

$$\boxed{\mathbf{A}} \equiv \boxed{L_{W_{t+1}, w_t | w_{t-1}, W_{t-2}} L_{W_{t+1}, \overline{w}_t | w_{t-1}, W_{t-2}}^{-1}}$$

$$= L_{W_{t+1} | w_t, X_t^*} D'_{w_t | w_{t-1}, X_t^*} D_{\overline{w}_t | w_{t-1}, X_t^*}^{-1} L_{W_{t+1} | \overline{w}_t, X_t^*}^{-1} \cdot$$

- Eliminate $L_{X_t^* | \overline{w}_{t-1}, W_{t-2}}$ using last two equations

$$\boxed{\mathbf{B}} \equiv \boxed{L_{W_{t+1}, w_t | \overline{w}_{t-1}, W_{t-2}} L_{W_{t+1}, \overline{w}_t | \overline{w}_{t-1}, W_{t-2}}^{-1}}$$

$$= L_{W_{t+1} | w_t, X_t^*} D_{w_t | \overline{w}_{t-1}, X_t^*} D_{\overline{w}_t | \overline{w}_{t-1}, X_t^*}^{-1} L_{W_{t+1} | \overline{w}_t, X_t^*}^{-1} \cdot$$

- Eliminate $L_{W_{t+1} | \overline{w}_t, X_t^*}^{-1}$,

$$\boxed{\mathbf{A}\mathbf{B}^{-1}} = L_{W_{t+1} | w_t, X_t^*} D_{w_t, \overline{w}_t, w_{t-1}, \overline{w}_{t-1}, X_t^*} L_{W_{t+1} | w_t, X_t^*}^{-1},$$

with diagonal matrix,

$$D_{w_t, \overline{w}_t, w_{t-1}, \overline{w}_{t-1}, X_t^*}$$
$$= D_{w_t | w_{t-1}, X_t^*} D_{\overline{w}_t | w_{t-1}, X_t^*}^{-1} D_{\overline{w}_t | \overline{w}_{t-1}, X_t^*} D_{w_t | \overline{w}_{t-1}, X_t^*}^{-1}.$$

Eigenvalue-eigenvector decomposition of observed $\boxed{\mathbf{AB}^{-1}}$

$$\boxed{\mathbf{AB}^{-1}} = L_{W_{t+1} | w_t, X_t^*} D_{w_t, \overline{w}_t, w_{t-1}, \overline{w}_{t-1}, X_t^*} L_{W_{t+1} | w_t, X_t^*}^{-1},$$

- eigenvalues: diagonal entry in $D_{w_t, \overline{w}_t, w_{t-1}, \overline{w}_{t-1}, X_t^*}$,

$$\left(D_{w_t, \overline{w}_t, w_{t-1}, \overline{w}_{t-1}, X_t^*} \right)_{j,j}$$
$$= \frac{f_{W_t | W_{t-1}, X_t^*}(w_t | w_{t-1}, j) f_{W_t | W_{t-1}, X_t^*}(\overline{w}_t | \overline{w}_{t-1}, j)}{f_{W_t | W_{t-1}, X_t^*}(\overline{w}_t | w_{t-1}, j) f_{W_t | W_{t-1}, X_t^*}(w_t | \overline{w}_{t-1}, j)}.$$

Assume: (Unique eigendecomposition) $\left(D_{w_t, \overline{w}_t, w_{t-1}, \overline{w}_{t-1}, X_t^*} \right)_{j,j}$ are distinctive,

- eigenvector: column in $L_{W_{t+1} | w_t, X_t^*}$ (normalized because sums to 1).

Hence, $L_{W_{t+1} | w_t, X_t^*}$ is identified (up to the value of x_t^*). Any permutation of eigenvectors yields same decomposition.

To pin-down the value of x_t^*: need to "order" eigenvectors,

- $f_{W_{t+1} | W_t, X_t^*}(\cdot | w_t, x_t^*)$ for any w_t is identified up to value of x_t^*. So to pin-down:
- Assume: (Normalization) there is *known* functional,

$$h(w_t, x_t^*) \equiv G[\, f_{W_{t+1} | W_t, X_t^*}(\cdot | w_t, \cdot)\,] \text{ is monotonic in } x_t^*.$$

$G[f]$ may be mean, mode, median, other quantile of f. Then set $x_t^* = G[\, f_{W_{t+1} | W_t, X_t^*}(\cdot | w_t, \cdot)\,]$.

- *Note*: in unobserved heterogeneity case $(X_t^* = X^*, \forall t)$, it is enough to identify $f_{W_{t+1}|W_t, X_t^*}$.

Main results

- **Theorem 1.** Under assumptions above, the density $f_{W_{t+1}, W_t, W_{t-1}, W_{t-2}, W_{t-3}}$ uniquely determines $f_{W_t, X_t^*|W_{t-1}, X_{t-1}^*}$.

- **Corollary 1.** With stationarity, the density $f_{W_{t+1}, W_t, W_{t-1}, W_{t-2}}$ uniquely determines $f_{W_2, X_2^*|W_1, X_1^*}$.

- For specific *DDC models* (IO, labor, health), we can use existing arguments from Magnac and Thesmar (2002) and Bajari *et al.* (2007) to argue identification of utility functions, once $W_t, X_t^*|W_{t-1}, X_{t-1}^*$ is known.

Bibliography

Bajari, P., V. Chernozhukov, H. Hong and D. Nekipelov (2007): "Nonparametric and Semiparametric Analysis of a Dynamic Game Model," Manuscript, University of Minnesota.

Carroll, R., X. Chen and Y. Hu (2009): "Identification and estimation of nonlinear models using two samples with nonclassical measurement errors," *J. Nonparametr. Stat.*, forthcoming.

Fernandez-Villaverde, J. and J. Rubio-Ramirez (2007): "Estimating Macroeconomic Models: A Likelihood Approach," *Rev. Econ. Stud.*, **74**, 1059–1087.

Flury, T. and N. Shephard (2008): "Bayesian inference based only on simulated likelihood: particle filter analysis of dynamic economic models," manuscript, Oxford University.

Hu, Y. (2008): "Identification and Estimation of Nonlinear Models with Misclassification Error Using Instrumental Variables: a General Solution," *J. Econometrics*, **144**, 27–61.

Hu, Y. and S. Schennach (2008): "Instrumental variable treatment of nonclassical measurement error models," *Econometrica*, **76**, 195–216.

Hu, Y. and M. Shum (2008): "Nonparametric Identification of Dynamic Models with Unobserved State Variables," Jonhs Hopkins University, Dept. of Economics working paper #543.

Magnac, T. and D. Thesmar (2002): "Identifying Dynamic Discrete Decision Processes," *Econometrica*, **70**, 801–816.

Pakes, A. (1986): "Patents as Options: Some Estimates of the Value of Holding European Patent Stocks," *Econometrica*, **54**(4), 755–84.

Rubin, D. (1988): "Using the SIR Algorithm to Simulate Posterior Distributions," in *Bayesian Statistics 3*, eds. J. Bernardo, M. DeGroot, D. Lindley and A. Smith. Oxford University Press.

Chapter 5

Dynamic Games

5.1 Econometrics of Dynamic Oligopoly Models

In describing the estimation of dynamic oligopoly models, I will focus on how these models fit into the framework of the single-agent dynamic optimization models (which we have discussed in quite exhaustive detail). In particular, we will see how the various estimation methods that we have discussed for single-agent models — namely, the (i) nested fixed-point and (ii) Hotz–Miller style conditional choice probabilities (CCP) approaches — can be extended to the case of dynamic games, in which multiple agents solve simultaneous and interconnected dynamic optimization problems.

In a certain sense, one can view the goal of the empirical dynamic games literature to develop a "multiplayer version of Rust's bus engine replacement model". In order for the single-agent-type method to work in the dynamic games setting, some assumptions have to be made, both in terms of the theoretical aspects of the model (restrictions on players' behavior), as well as the econometric specification of the model (particularly, the specifications of the *structural errors* in the model.

In the theoretical aspects, the typical assumption is that firms are playing a *Markov-perfect equilibrium*; see Ericson and Pakes (1995). In the econometric specification, the most common framework is that the players are playing a "game with incomplete information," in which each player's idiosyncratic utility shocks (which are the structural errors in the model), are the *private information* of each player. We will go into each of these components in turn.

5.2   Theoretical Features

Since I am not a theorist, I will simply describe the assumptions that are made, without commenting much on deeper theoretical matters. The Ericson and Pakes (1995) paper fills in many theoretical details.

Consider a simple two-firm model, with firms $i = 1, 2$, and periods $t = 1, 2, \ldots$.

Let x_{1t}, x_{2t}, denote the state variables for each firm in each period. Let q_{1t}, q_{2t} denote the control (decision) variables. Example: in a dynamic investment model, the x's are capacity levels, and q's are incremental changes to capacity in each period. Assume that $x_{it+1} = g(x_{it}, q_{it})$, $i = 1, 2$, so that next period's state is a deterministic function of this period's state and control variable.

Firm i (=1, 2) chooses a sequence $q_{i1}, q_{i2}, q_{i3}, \ldots$ to maximize its discounted profits:

$$\sum_{t=0}^{\infty} \beta^t \Pi \left(x_{1t}, x_{2t}, q_{1t}, q_{2t} \right),$$

where $\Pi(\cdots)$ denotes single-period profits. Because the two firms are duopolists, and they must make these choices recognizing that their choices can affect their rival's choices. We want to consider a dynamic equilibrium of such a model, when (roughly speaking) each firm's sequence of q's is a "best-response" to its rival's sequence.

A firm's strategy in period t, q_{it}, can potentially depend on the whole "history" of the game ($\mathcal{H}_{t-1} \equiv \{x_{1t'}, x_{2t'}, q_{1t'}, q_{2t'}\}_{t'=0,\ldots,t-1}$), and well as on the time period t itself. This becomes quickly intractable, so we usually make some simplifying regularity conditions:

- Firms employ *stationary* strategies: so that strategies are not explicitly a function of time t (i.e., they depend on time only indirectly, through the history $\mathcal{H}_{t-1}$). Given stationarity, we will drop the t subscript, and use primes $'$ to denote next-period values.

- A dimension-reducing assumption is usually made: for example, we might assume that q_{it} depends only on x_{1t}, x_{2t}, which are the "payoff-relevant" state variables which directly affect firm i's profits in period i. This is usually called a "Markov" assumption. With this assumption $q_{it} = q_i(x_{1t}, x_{2t})$, for all t.
- Furthermore, we may also make a *symmetry* assumption, that each firm employs an identical strategy assumption. This implies that $q_1(x_{1t}, x_{2t}) = q_2(x_{2t}, x_{1t})$.

To characterize the equilibrium further, assume we have an equilibrium strategy function $q^*(\cdot, \cdot)$. For each firm i, then, and at each state vector x_1, x_2, this optimal policy must satisfy Bellman's equation, in order for the strategy to constitute subgame-perfect behavior:

$$q^*(x_1, x_2) = \mathrm{argmax}_q \big\{ \Pi(x_1, x_2, q, q^*(x_2, x_1)) $$
$$+ \beta V\left(x_1' = g(x_1, q), x_2' = g(x_2, q^*(x_2, x_1)))\right) \big\}, \quad (5.1)$$

from firm 1's perspective, and similarly for firm 2. $V(\cdot, \cdot)$ is the value function, defined recursively at all possible state vectors x_1, x_2 via the Bellman equation:

$$V(x_1, x_2) = \max_q \big\{ \Pi(x_1, x_2, q, q^*(x_2, x_1)) $$
$$+ \beta V\left(x_1' = g(x_1, q), x_2' = g(x_2, q^*(x_2, x_1)))\right) \big\}. \quad (5.2)$$

I have described the simplest case; given this structure, it is clear that the following extensions are straightforward:

- More than two firms.
- Cross-effects: $x_i' = g(x_i, x_{-i}, q_i, q_{-i})$.
- Stochastic evolution: $x_i'|x_i, q_i$ is a random variable. In this case, replace last term of Bellman equation by $E[V(x_1', x_2')|x_1, x_2, q, q_2 = q^*(x_2, x_1)]$.
  This expectation denotes player 1's *equilibrium beliefs* about the evolution of x_1 and x_2 (equilibrium in the sense that he assumes that player 2 plays the equilibrium strategy $q^*(x_2, x_1)$).
- > 2 firms.

- Firms employ asymmetric strategies, so that $q_1(x_1, x_2) \neq q_2(x_2, x_1)$.

5.2.1   Computation of dynamic equilibrium

In principle, one could estimate a dynamic games model, given time series of $\{x_t, q_t\}$ for both firms, by using a nested fixed-point estimation algorithm, similar to what Rust originally proposed for his bus-engine replacement model. In the outer loop, we loop over different values of the parameters θ, and then in the inner loop, you compute the equilibrium of the dynamic game (in the way described above) for each value of θ. Examples of empirical dynamic games paper which utilize such a NFXP estimation procedure are: Goettler and Gordon (2011), Gallant, Hong, and Khwaja (2009).

Computing the equilibrium strategy $q^*(\cdots)$ consists in iterating over the Bellman equation (5.1). However, the problem is more complicated than the single-agent case for several reasons.

For one thing, the value function itself depends on the optimal strategy function $q^*(\cdots)$, via the assumption that the rival firm is always using the optimal strategy. So value iteration procedure is more complicated:

1. Start with initial guess $V^0(x_1, x_2)$.
2. If q's are continuous controls, we must solve for $q_1^0 \equiv q^0(x_1, x_2)$ and $q_2^0 \equiv q^0(x_2, x_1)$ to satisfy the system of first-order conditions (here subscripts denotes partial derivatives),

$$0 = \Pi_3\left(x_1, x_2, q_1^0, q_2^0\right) + \beta V_1^0\left(g\left(x_1, q_1^0\right), g\left(x_2, q_2^0\right)\right) \cdot g_2\left(x_1, q_1^0\right),$$
$$0 = \Pi_3\left(x_2, x_1, q_2^0, q_1^0\right) + \beta V_1^0\left(g\left(x_2, q_2^0\right), g\left(x_1, q_1^0\right)\right) \cdot g_2\left(x_2, q_2^0\right).$$
$$(5.3)$$

For the discrete control case:

$$q^0 = \operatorname{argmax}_{q \in \mathcal{Q}} \left\{\Pi\left(x_1, x_2, q, q_2^0\right) + \beta V^0\left(g\left(x_1, q\right), g\left(x_2, q_2^0\right)\right)\right\},$$
$$q_2^0 = \operatorname{argmax}_{q \in \mathcal{Q}} \left\{\Pi\left(x_2, x_1, q, q_1^0\right) + \beta V^0\left(g\left(x_2, q\right), g\left(x_1, q_1^0\right)\right)\right\}.$$
$$(5.4)$$

3. Update the next iteration of the value function:

$$V^1(x_1, x_2) = \left\{ \Pi\left(x_1, x_2, q_1^0, q_2^0\right) + \beta V^0\left(g\left(x_1, q_1^0\right), g\left(x_2, q_2^0\right)\right) \right\}.$$
(5.5)

Note: this and the previous step must be done at all points (x_1, x_2) in the discretized grid. As usual, use interpolation or approximation to obtain $V^1(\cdots)$ at points not on the grid.

4. Stop when $\sup_{x_1, x_2} \|V^{i+1}(x_1, x_2) - V^i(x_1, x_2)\| \leq \epsilon$.

Second, there is an inherent "Curse of dimensionality" with dynamic games, because the dimensionality of the state vector (x_1, x_2) is equal to the number of firms. (For instance, if you want to discretize 1,000 pts in one dimension, you have to discretize at 1,000,000 pts to maintain the same fineness in two dimensions!)

Some papers provide computational methods to circumvent this problem (Keane and Wolpin, 1994; Pakes and McGuire, 2001; Imai, Jain, and Ching, 2009). Generally, these papers advocate only computing the value function at a (small) subset of the state points for each iteration, and then approximating the value function at the rest of the state points using values calculated during previous iterations.

5.3 Games with "Incomplete Information"

What about extending the Hotz–Miller-type insights to facilitate estimation of dynamic oligopoly models? Indeed, this has become the dominant estimation approach for these models. Papers which develop these ideas include: Bajari, Benkard, and Levin (2007), Pesendorfer and Schmidt-Dengler (2008), Aguirregabiria and Mira (2007), Pakes, Ostrovsky, and Berry (2007). Applications include: Collard-Wexler (2006), Ryan (2012), and Dunne *et al.* (2006). See survey in Pakes (2008), Section 3.

Here I outline the general setting, which can be considered a multiagent version of Rust setup.

Let $\vec{X}$ and $\vec{q}$ denote the N-vector of firms' state variables, and actions. $\{\vec{X}, \vec{q}\}$ jointly evolve (in equilibrium) as a first-order Markov process We make the assumptions of *symmetric*, which implies that firms are identical, up to the current values of their state variables, and idiosyncratic utility shocks.

Data directly tell you: the choice probabilities (distribution of $q_1, q_2 | x_1, x_2$); state transitions: (joint distribution of $x_1' x_2' | x_1, x_2, q_2, q_2$).

Random utility assumption: firm i's current utility, given her action q_i and her utility shocks ϵ_{i,q_i} is:

$$U(\vec{X}, q_i, \vec{q}_{-i}; \theta) + \epsilon_{i,q_i}.$$

All utility shocks are *private information* of firm i. Also, they are identically and independently distributed (i.i.d.) across firms, and across actions (exactly like the logit errors in Rust's framework).

Because of these assumptions: each firm's period t shocks affect only its period t actions; they do not affect opponents' actions, nor do they affect actions in other periods $t' \neq t$.

In single-agent case, this distinction of private vs. public information is nonsensical. But in multiagent context, it is crucial. Consider several alternatives:

- All the shocks are publicly observed each period, but not observed by econometrician: essentially, we are in the "unobserved state variable" world of the last set of lecture notes, except that in multiagent context, each firm's actions in each period depend on *all* the shocks of all the firms in that period. Conditional on $\vec{X}$, firms' decisions will be correlated, which raises difficulties for estimation.

- Shocks are private information, but *serially correlated* over time: now firms can learn about their opponents' shocks through their actions, and their beliefs may evolve in complicated fashion. Also, firms may strategically try to influence their rivals' beliefs about their shocks ("signalling"). This causes complications even from a theoretical modeling perspective.

- Shocks are unobserved by both firms and econometrician. In this case, they are nonstructural errors and are useless from the point of view of generating more randomness in the model relative to the data.

In symmetric Markov-perfect equilibrium, firms' optimal policy function takes the form $q_i = q^*(\vec{X}, \epsilon_i)$. Corresponding CCP (conditional choice probability): $P(q_i|\vec{X})$ (randomness in ϵ_i). These can be estimated from data. State variables evolve via Markovian law-of-motion $\vec{X}'|\vec{X}, \vec{q}$. This can also be estimated from the data. In other words, the transition kernel, in equilibrium, for the process $\{\vec{X}, \vec{q}\}$ can be factored into the product of the conditional choice probabilities times the transition probabilities for the state variables X:

$$P(\vec{X}', \vec{q}'|\vec{X}, \vec{q}) = \prod_i P(X_i'|\vec{X}, \vec{q}) \cdot P(q_i'|\vec{X}).$$

Subsequently, choice-specific value functions for firm i (identical for all firms) can be forward-simulated:

$$\tilde{V}(\vec{X}, q_i = 1; \theta)$$
$$= E_{\vec{d}_{-i}|\vec{X}} u(\vec{X}, q_i = 1, \vec{q}_{-i}; \theta) + \beta E_{\vec{X}'|\vec{X}, \vec{q}=(q_i, \vec{q}_{-i})} E_{\vec{q}'|\vec{X}'} E_{\epsilon'|q_i', \vec{X}'}$$
$$\times \left[u(\vec{X}', \vec{q}'; \theta) + \epsilon_{q'}' + \beta E_{\vec{X}''|\vec{X}', \vec{q}'} E_{\vec{q}''|\vec{X}''} E_{\epsilon''|q_i'', \vec{X}''} \right.$$
$$\times \left. \left[u(\vec{X}'', \vec{q}''; \theta) + \epsilon_{q''}'' + \beta \cdots \right] \right]. \tag{5.6}$$

When $\vec{X}$ is finite, the matrix representation of value function can also be used here.

If the private information shocks are assumed to be completely exogenous and distributed type I extreme value, then the predicted choice probabilities take the familiar multinomial logit (MNL) form:

$$\tilde{P}(q_i = 1|\vec{X}) = \frac{\exp(\tilde{V}(\vec{X}, q_i = 1; \theta))}{\exp(\tilde{V}(\vec{X}, q_i = 1; \theta)) + \exp(\tilde{V}(\vec{X}, q_i = 0; \theta))}.$$

Bibliography

Aguirregabiria, V. and P. Mira (2007): "Sequential Estimation of Dynamic Discrete Games," *Econometrica*, **75**, 1–53.

Bajari, P., L. Benkard and J. Levin (2007): "Estimating Dynamic Models of Imperfect Competition," *Econometrica*, **75**, 1331–1370.

Collard-Wexler, A. (2006): "Demand Fluctuations and Plant Turnover in the Ready-to-Mix Concrete Industry," manuscript, New York University.

Dunne, T., S. Klimer, M. Roberts and D. Xu (2006): "Entry and Exit in Geographic Markets," manuscript, Penn State University.

Ericson, R. and A. Pakes (1995): "Markov-Perfect Industry Dynamics: A Framework for Empirical Work," *Rev. Econ. Stud.*, **62**, 53–82.

Gallant, R., H. Hong and A. Khwaja (2009): "Estimating a Dynamic Oligopolistic Game with Serially Correlated Unobserved Production Costs," manuscript, Duke University.

Goettler, R. and B. Gordon (2011): "Does AMD SPur Intel to Innovate More?," *J. Polit. Econ.*, **119**, 1141–1200.

Imai, S., N. Jain and A. Ching (2009): "Bayesian Estimation of Dynamic Discrete Choice Models," *Econometrica*, **77**, 1865–1899.

Keane, M. and K. Wolpin (1994): "The Solution and Estimation of Discrete Choice Dynamic Programming Models by Simulation and Interpolation: Monte Carlo Evidence," *Rev. Econ. Stat.*, **76**, 648–672.

Pakes, A. (2008): "Theory and Empirical Work in Imperfectly Competitive Markets," Fisher-Schultz Lecture at 2005 Econometric Society World Congress (London, England).

Pakes, A. and P. McGuire (2001): "Stochastic Algorithms, Symmetric Markov Perfect Equilibrium, and the 'Curse' of Dimensionality," *Econometrica*, **69**, 1261–1282.

Pakes, A., M. Ostrovsky and S. Berry (2007): "Simple Estimators for the Parameters of Discrete Dynamic Games (with Entry Exit Examples)," *RAND J. Econ.*, **38**, 373–399.

Pesendorfer, M. and P. Schmidt-Dengler (2008): "Asymptotic Least Squares Estimators for Dynamic Games," *Rev. Econ. Stud.*, **75**, 901–928.

Ryan, S. (2012): "The Costs of Environmental Regulation in a Concentrated Industry," *Econometrica*, **80**, 1019–1061.

Chapter 6

Auction Models

Goal of empirical work:

- We observe bids $b_1, \ldots, b_n$, and we want to recover valuations $v_1, \ldots, v_n$.
- Why? Analogously to demand estimation, we can evaluate the "market power" of bidders, as measured by the margin $v - p$. Interesting policy question: how fast does margin decrease as n (number of bidders) increases?
- Useful for the optimal design of auctions:

  1. What is auction format which would maximize seller revenue?
  2. What value for reserve price would maximize seller revenue?

- Methodology: identification, nonparametric estimation.

6.1 Parametric Estimation: Laffont–Ossard–Vuong (1995)

In this section, we study the parametric estimation of structural first-price auction models, via the paper by Laffont, Ossard, and Vuong (1995).

- Structural estimation of 1PA model, in IPV context.
- Example of a parametric approach to estimation.
- Another exercise in simulation estimation.

MODEL

- I bidders
- Information structure is IPV: valuations v^i, $i = 1, \ldots, I$ are i.i.d. from $F(\cdot|z_l, \theta)$ where l indexes auctions, and z_l are characteristics of lth auctions
- θ is parameter vector of interest, and goal of estimation.
- p^0 denotes "reserve price": bid is rejected if $< p^0$.
- Dutch auction: strategically identical to first-price sealed bid auction.

Equilibrium bidding strategy is:

$$b^i = e\left(v^i, I, p^0, F\right) = \begin{cases} v^i - \dfrac{\int_{p^0}^{v^i} F(x)^{I-1} dx}{F(v^i)^{I-1}} & \text{if } v^i > p^0, \\ 0 & \text{otherwise.} \end{cases} \quad (6.1)$$

Note: (1) $b^i(v^i = p^0) = p^0$; (2) strictly increasing in v^i.

Dataset: only observe *winning bid* b_l^w for each auction l. Because bidders with lower bids never have a chance to bid in Dutch auction.

Given monotonicity, the winning bid $b^w = e\left(v_{(I)}, I, p^0, F\right)$, where $v_{(I)} \equiv \max_i v^i$ (the highest order statistic out of the I valuations).

Furthermore, the CDF of $v_{(I)}$ is $F(\cdot|z_l, \theta)^I$, with corresponding density $I \cdot F^{I-1} f$.

Goal is to estimate θ by (roughly speaking) matching the winning bid in each auction l to its expectation.

Expected winning bid is (for simplicity, drop z_l and θ now)

$$E_{v_{(I)} > p^0}(b^w) = \int_{p^0}^{\infty} e\left(v_{(I)}, I, p^0, F\right) I \cdot F(v|\theta)^{I-1} f(v|\theta) dv$$

$$= I \int_{p^0}^{\infty} \left(v - \dfrac{\int_{p^0}^{v} F(x)^{I-1} dx}{F(v)^{I-1}}\right) F(v|\theta)^{I-1} f(v|\theta) dv$$

$$= I \int_{p^0}^{\infty} \left(v \cdot F(v)^{I-1} - \int_{p^0}^{\infty} F(x)^{I-1} dx\right) f(v) dv. \quad (*)$$

If we were to estimate by simulated nonlinear least squares, we would proceed by finding θ to minimize the sum-of-squares between the observed winning bids and the predicted winning bid, given by expression (*) above. Since (*) involves complicated integrals, we would simulate (*), for each parameter vector θ.

How would this be done:

- Draw valuations v^s, $s = 1, \ldots, S$ i.i.d. according to $f(v|\theta)$. This can be done by drawing $u_1, \ldots, u_S$ i.i.d. from the $U[0,1]$ distribution, then transform each draw:

$$v_s = F^{-1}(u_s|\theta).$$

- For each simulated valuation v_s, compute integrand $\mathcal{V}_s = v_s F(v_s|\theta)^{I-1} - \int_{p^0}^{v_s} F(x|\theta)^{I-1} dx$. (Second term can also be simulated, but one-dimensional integral is that very hard to compute.)
- Approximate the expected winning bid as $\frac{1}{S} \sum_s \mathcal{V}_s$.

However, the authors do not do this — they propose a more elegant solution. In particular, they simplify the simulation procedure for the expected winning bid by appealing to the **Revenue Equivalence Theorem (RET)**: an important result for auctions where bidders' signals are independent, and the model is symmetric. (See Myerson, 1981; this statement is due to Klemperer, 1999.)

Theorem 1 (Revenue Equivalence). *Assume each of N risk-neutral bidders has a privately-known signal X independently drawn from a common distribution F that is strictly increasing and atomless on its support $[\underline{X}, \bar{X}]$. Any auction mechanism which is (i) efficient in awarding the object to the bidder with the highest signal with probability one; and (ii) leaves any bidder with the lowest signal $\underline{X}$ with zero surplus yields the same expected revenue for the seller, and results in a bidder with signal x making the same expected payment.*

From a mechanism design point of view, auctions are complicated because they are multiagent problems, in which a given agent's payoff can depend on the reports of all the agents. However, in the independent signal case, there is no gain (in terms of stronger incentives) in making any given agent's payoff depend on her rivals' reports, so that a symmetric auction with independent signal essentially boils down to independent contracts offered to each of the agents individually.

Furthermore, in any efficient auction, the probability that a given agent with a signal x wins is the same (and, in fact, equals $F(x)^{N-1}$). This implies that each bidder's expected surplus function (as a function of his signal) is the same, and therefore that the expected payment schedule is the same.

By RET:

- Expected revenue in 1PA same as expected revenue in 2PA.
- Expected revenue in 2PA is $Ev^{(I-1)}$.
- With reserve price, expected revenue in 2PA is $E\max(v^{(I-1)}, p^0)$ (*Note*: with IPV structure, reserve price r screens out same subset of valuations $v \leq r$ in both 1PA and 2PA).

Hence, we have that

$$Eb^*(v_{(I)}) = E\left[\max\left(v_{(I-1)}, p^0\right)\right],$$

which is insanely easy to simulate:

For each parameter vector θ, and each auction l.

- For each simulation draw $s = 1, \ldots, S$:

  — Draw $v_1^s, \ldots, v_{I_l}^s$: vector of simulated valuations for auction l (which had I_l participants).
  — Sort the draws in ascending order: $v_{1:I_l}^s < \cdots < v_{I_l:I_l}^s$
  — Set $b_l^{w,s} = v_{I-1_l:I_l}$ (i.e., the second-highest valuation).
  — If $b_l^{w,s} < p_l^0$, set $b_l^{w,s} = p_l^0$. (i.e., $b_l^{w,s} = \max\left(v_{I-1_l:I_l}^s, p_l^0\right)$).

- Approximate $E(b_l^w; \theta) = \frac{1}{S}\sum_s b_l^{w,s}$.

Estimate θ by simulated nonlinear least squares:

$$\min_{\theta} \frac{1}{L}\sum_{l=1}^{L}(b_l^w - E(b_l^w; \theta))^2.$$

Results.

Remarks:

- Problem: bias when number of simulation draws S is fixed (as number of auctions $L \to \infty$). Propose bias correction estimator, which is consistent and asymptotic normal under these conditions.
- This clever methodology is useful for independent value models: works for all cases where revenue equivalence theorem holds.
- Does not work for affiliated value models (including common value models).

6.2 Nonparametric Estimation: Guerre–Perrigne–Vuong (2000)

The recent emphasis in the empirical literature is on *nonparametric* identification and estimation of auction models. Motivation is to estimate bidders' unobserved valuations, while avoiding parametric assumption (as in the LOV paper). The seminal paper in this literature is Guerre, Perrigne, and Vuong (2000).

- Start with first-order condition:

$$b'(x) = (x - b(x)) \cdot (n-1) \frac{F(x)^{n-2} f(x)}{F(x)^{n-1}}$$

$$= (x - b(x)) \cdot (n-1) \frac{f(x)}{F(x)}. \tag{6.2}$$

- Now, note that because equilibrium bidding function $b(x)$ is just a monotone increasing function of the valuation x, the change of variables formulas yield that (take $b_i \equiv b(x_i)$)

$$G(b_i) = F(x_i)$$

$$g(b_i) = f(x_i) \cdot 1/b'(x_i).$$

Hence, substituting the above into Eq. (6.2):

$$\frac{1}{g(b_i)} = (n-1) \frac{x_i - b_i}{G(b_i)},$$

$$\Leftrightarrow x_i = b_i + \frac{G(b_i)}{(n-1)g(b_i)}. \tag{6.3}$$

Everything on the RHS of the preceding equation is observed: the equilibrium bid CDF G and density g can be estimated directly from the data *nonparametrically*. Assuming a dataset consisting of T n-bidder auctions:

$$\hat{g}(b) \approx \frac{1}{T \cdot n} \sum_{t=1}^{T} \sum_{i=1}^{n} \frac{1}{h} \mathcal{K} \left(\frac{b - b_{it}}{h} \right)$$

$$\hat{G}(b) \approx \frac{1}{T \cdot n} \sum_{t=1}^{T} \sum_{i=1}^{n} \mathbf{1}(b_{it} \leq b). \tag{6.4}$$

The first is a *kernel density estimate* of bid density. The second is the *empirical distribution function* (EDF).

- In the above, $\mathcal{K}$ is a "kernel function." A kernel function is a function satisfying the following conditions:

  1. It is a probability density function, i.e.: $\int_{-\infty}^{+\infty} \mathcal{K}(d) du = 1$, and $\mathcal{K}(u) \geq 0$ for all u.
  2. It is symmetric around zero: $\mathcal{K}(u) = \mathcal{K}(-u)$.
  3. h is bandwidth: described in the following text.
  4. Examples:

     (a) $\mathcal{K}(u) = \phi(u)$ (standard normal density function);
     (b) $\mathcal{K}(u) = \frac{1}{2} \mathbf{1}(|u| \leq 1)$ (uniform kernel);
     (b) $\mathcal{K}(u) = \frac{3}{4}(1 - u^2) \mathbf{1}(|u| \leq 1)$ (Epanechnikov kernel).

- To get some intuition for the kernel estimate of $\hat{g}(b)$, consider the histogram:

$$h(b) = \frac{1}{Tn} \sum_{t} \sum_{i} \mathbf{1}(b_{it} \in [b - \epsilon, b + \epsilon]),$$

for some small $\epsilon > 0$. The histogram at b, $h(b)$ is the frequency with which the observed bids land within an ϵ-neighborhood of b.

- In comparison, the kernel estimate of $\hat{g}(b)$ replaces $\mathbf{1}(b_{it} \in [b - \epsilon, b + \epsilon])$ with $\frac{1}{h} \mathcal{K} \left(\frac{b - b_{it}}{h} \right)$. This is:

  — always ≥ 0,
  — takes large values for b_{it} close to b; small values (or zero) for b_{it} far from b,

— takes values in $\mathbb{R}+$ (can be much larger than 1),
— h is bandwidth, which blows up $\frac{1}{h}\mathcal{K}\left(\frac{b-b_{it}}{h}\right)$: when it is smaller, then this quantity becomes larger.

Think of h as measuring the "neighborhood size" (like ϵ in the histogram). When $T \to \infty$, then we can make h smaller and smaller.

Bias/variance tradeoff.

— Roughly speaking, then, $\hat{g}(b)$ is a "smoothed" histogram.

• For $\hat{G}(b)$, recall definition of the *CDF*:

$$G(\tilde{b}) = Pr(b \leq \tilde{b}).$$

The EDF measures these probabilities by the (within-sample) frequency of the events.

• Hence, the IPV first-price auction model is *nonparametrically identified*. For each observed bid b_i, the corresponding valuation $x_i = b^{-1}(b_i)$ can be recovered as:

$$\hat{x}_i = b_i + \frac{\hat{G}(b_i)}{(n-1)\hat{g}(b_i)}. \tag{6.5}$$

Hence, GPV recommend a two-step approach to estimating the valuation distribution $f(x)$:

1. In first step, estimate $G(b)$ and $g(b)$ nonparametrically, using Eq. (6.4).
2. In second step, estimate $f(x)$ by using kernel density estimator of recovered valuations:

$$\hat{f}(x) \approx \frac{1}{T \cdot n} \sum_{t=1}^{T} \sum_{i=1}^{n} \frac{1}{h}\mathcal{K}\left(\frac{x - \hat{x}_{it}}{h}\right). \tag{6.6}$$

Note that identification continues to hold, even when only the highest-bid in each auction is observed. Specifically, if only $b_{n:n}$ is observed, we can estimate $G_{n:n}$, the CDF of the maximum bid, from the data. Note that the relationship between the CDF of the maximum bid and the marginal CDF of an equilibrium bid is,

$$G_{n:n}(b) = G(b)^n,$$

implying that $G(b)$ can be recovered from knowledge of $G_{n:n}(b)$. Once $G(b)$ is recovered, the corresponding density $g(b)$ can also be recovered, and we could solve Eq. (6.5) for every b to obtain the inverse bid function.

Athey and Haile (2002) contains a comprehensive collection of nonparametric identification results for a variety of auction models (first-price, second-price) under a variety of assumption on the information structure (symmetry, asymmetry). One focus in their paper is on situations when only a subset of the bids submitted in an auction are available to a researcher.

6.3 Affiliated Values Models

Can this methodology be extended to affiliated values models (including common value models)?

However, based on Laffont and Vuong (1996) nonidentification result: from observation of bids in n-bidder auctions, the affiliated private value (PV) model (i.e., a PV model where valuations are dependent across bidders) is indistinguishable from a common value (CV) model.

- Intuitively, all you identify from observed bid data is joint density of $b_1, \ldots, b_n$. In particular, can recover the correlation structure amongst the bids. But correlation of bids in an auction could be due to both affiliated PV, or to CV.

6.3.1 Affiliated PV models

Li, Perrigne, and Vuong (2002) proceed to consider nonparametric identification and estimation of the affiliated PV model. In this model, valuations $x_i, \ldots, x_n$ are drawn from some joint distribution (and there can be arbitrary correlation amongst them).

First-order condition for equilibrium bid in affiliated private values case:

$$b'(x) = (x - b(x)) \cdot \frac{f_{y_i|x_i}(x|x)}{F_{y_i|x_i}(x|x)}; \quad y_i \equiv \max_{j \neq i} x_i, \qquad (6.7)$$

where $y_i \equiv \max_{j \neq i} x_i$ (highest among rivals' signals) and $b(\cdot)$ denotes the equilibrium bidding strategy.

Procedure similar to GPV can be used here to recover, for each bid b_i, the corresponding valuation $x_i = b^{-1}(b_i)$. Let b_i^* denote the maximum among bidder i's rivals bids: $b_i^* = \max_{j \neq i} b_j$. Then there is a monotonic transformation $b_i^* = b(y_i)$ so that, as before, we exploit the following change of variable formulas:

- $$G_{b^*|b}(b|b) = F_{y|x}(x|x),$$

- $$g_{b^*|b}(b|b) = f_{y|x}(x|x) \cdot 1/b'(x).$$

Note that the conditioning event $\{X = x\}$ (on RHS) is equivalent to $\{B = b\}$ (on LHS). To prepare what follows, we introduce n subscript (so we index distributions according to the number of bidders in the auction).

Li, Perrigne, and Vuong (2000) suggest nonparametric estimates of the form,

$$\hat{G}_n(b; b) = \frac{1}{T_n \times h \times n} \sum_{t=1}^{T} \sum_{i=1}^{n} K\left(\frac{b - b_{it}}{h}\right) \mathbf{1}\left(b_{it}^* < b, n_t = n\right),$$

$$\hat{g}_n(b; b) = \frac{1}{T_n \times h^2 \times n} \sum_{t=1}^{T} \sum_{i=1}^{n} \mathbf{1}(n_t = n) K\left(\frac{b - b_{it}}{h}\right) K\left(\frac{b - b_{it}^*}{h}\right).$$

$$(6.8)$$

Here h and h are bandwidths and $K(\cdot)$ is a kernel. $\hat{G}_n(b; b)$ and $\hat{g}_n(b; b)$ are nonparametric estimates of,

$$G_n(b; b) \equiv G_n(b|b)g_n(b) = \frac{\partial}{\partial b} \Pr(B_{it}^* \leq m, B_{it} \leq b)|_{m=b}$$

and

$$g_n(b; b) \equiv g_n(b|b)g_n(b) = \frac{\partial^2}{\partial m \partial b} \Pr(B_{it}^* \leq m, B_{it} \leq b)|_{m=b},$$

respectively, where $g_n(\cdot)$ is the marginal density of bids in equilibrium. Because

$$\frac{G_n(b; b)}{g_n(b; b)} = \frac{G_n(b|b)}{g_n(b|b)} \qquad (6.9)$$

$\frac{\hat{G}_n(b;b)}{\hat{g}_n(b;b)}$ is a consistent estimator of $\frac{G_n(b|b)}{g_n(b|b)}$. Hence, by evaluating $\hat{G}_n(\cdot,\cdot)$ and $\hat{g}_n(\cdot,\cdot)$ at each observed bid, we can construct a pseudo-sample of consistent estimates of the realizations of each $x_{it} = b^{-1}(b_{it})$ using Eq. (6.7):

$$\hat{x}_{it} = \frac{\hat{G}_n(b_{it}; b_{it})}{\hat{g}_n(b_{it}; b_{it})} + b_{it}. \tag{6.10}$$

Subsequently, joint distribution of $x_1, \ldots, x_n$ can be recovered as sample joint distribution of $\hat{x}_1, \ldots, \hat{x}_n$.

6.3.2   Common value models: Testing between CV and PV

Laffont–Vuong did not consider variation in n, the number of bidders.

In Haile, Hong, and Shum (2003), we explore how variation in n allows us to test for existence of CV.

Introduce notation:

$$v(x_i, x_i, n) = E[V_i | X_i = x_i, \max_{j \neq i} X_j = x_i, n].$$

This denotes the "value conditional on winning" (see theory notes, part 1). Recall the winner's curse: it implies that $v(x, x, n)$ is invariant to n for all x in a PV model but strictly decreasing in n for all x in a CV model (see theory notes, part 1).

Consider the first-order condition in the common value case:

$$b'(x, n) = (v(x, x, n) - b(x, n)) \cdot \frac{f_{y_i | x_i, n}(x|x)}{F_{y_i | x_i, n}(x|x)}; \quad y_i \equiv \max_{j \neq i} x_j.$$

Hence, the Li, Perrigne, and Vuong (2002) procedure from the previous section can be used to recover the "pseudovalue" $v(x_i, x_i, n)$ corresponding to each observed bid b_i. Note that we cannot recover $x_i = b^{-1}(b_i)$ itself from the first-order condition, but can recover $v(x_i, x_i, n)$. (This insight was also articulated in Hendricks, Pinkse, and Porter, 2003.)

In Haile, Hong, and Shum (2003), we use this intuition to develop a test for CV:

$$H_0 \text{ (PV)} : \ E\left[v(X,X;\underline{n})\right] = E\left[v(X,X;\underline{n}+1)\right]$$
$$= \cdots = E\left[v(X,X;\bar{n})\right],$$
$$H_1 \text{ (CV)} : \ E\left[v(X,X;\underline{n})\right] > E\left[v(X,X;\underline{n}+1)\right]$$
$$> \cdots > E\left[v(X,X;\bar{n})\right].$$

Problem: bias at boundaries in kernel estimation of pseudo-values. The bid density $g(b,b)$ is estimated inaccurately for bids close to the boundary of the empirical support of bids.

Solution: use *quantile-trimmed means*: $\mu_{n,\tau} = E[v(X,X;n)\mathbf{1}\{x_\tau < X < x_{1-\tau}\}]$
above $\Rightarrow$

$$H_0 \text{ (PV)} : \ \mu_{\underline{n},\tau} = \mu_{\underline{n}+1,\tau} = \cdots = \mu_{\bar{n},\tau},$$
$$H_1 \text{ (CV)} : \ \mu_{\underline{n},\tau} > \mu_{\underline{n}+1,\tau} > \cdots > \mu_{\bar{n},\tau}.$$

Theorem 3. Let $\hat{\mu}_{n,\tau} = \frac{1}{n\times T_n}\sum_{t=1}^{T_n}\sum_{i=1}^{n}\hat{v}_{it}\,\mathbf{1}\{b_{\tau,n} \le b_{it} \le b_{1-\tau,n}\}$ and assume [...conditions for kernel estimation...]. Then

(i) $\hat{\mu}_{n,\tau} \overset{p}{\longrightarrow} E[v(X,X,n)\,\mathbf{1}\{x_\tau < X < x_{1-\tau}\}]$;
(ii) $\sqrt{T_n h}\,(\hat{\mu}_{n,\tau} - \mu_{n,\tau}) \overset{d}{\longrightarrow} N(0,\omega_n)$, where

$$\omega_n = \left[\int\left(\int K(v)K(u+v)dv\right)^2 du\right]$$
$$\times \left[\frac{1}{n}\int_{F_b^{-1}(\tau)}^{F_b^{-1}(1-\tau)} \frac{G_n(b;b)^2}{g_n(b;b)^3} g_n(b)^2 db\right].$$

Test statistic: Now use standard multivariate one-sided LR test (Bartholomew, 1959) for normally distributed parameters $\hat{\mu}_{n,\tau}$

- $a_n = \frac{T_n h}{\omega_n}$ (inverse variance weights),

- $\bar{\mu} = \frac{\sum_{n=\underline{n}}^{\bar{n}} a_n \, \hat{\mu}_{n,\tau}}{\sum_{n=\underline{n}}^{\bar{n}} a_n}$ (MLE under null),

- $\mu_{\underline{n}}^*, \dots, \mu_{\bar{n}}^*$ solves

$$\min_{\mu_{\underline{n}}, \dots, \mu_{\bar{n}}} \sum_{n=\underline{n}}^{\bar{n}} a_n \left(\hat{\mu}_{n,\tau} - \mu_n \right)^2 \quad s.t. \quad \mu_{\underline{n}} \geq \mu_{\underline{n}+1} \geq \cdots \geq \mu_{\bar{n}}. \quad (13)$$

- $\bar{\chi}^2 = \sum_{n=\underline{n}}^{\bar{n}} a_n \left(\mu_{n,\tau}^* - \bar{\mu} \right)^2$,

  — distributed as mixture of χ_k^2 rv's, $k = 0, 1, \dots, \bar{n} - \underline{n}$,
  — mixing weights: $\Pr_{H_0}$ {soln to (13) has exactly k slack constraints} (obtain by simulation).

- estimate ω_n using asymptotic formula or with bootstrap

6.4 Haile–Tamer's "Incomplete" Model of English Auctions

Haile and Tamer (2003)

Consider an ascending auction where the bidders have independent private valuations. The number of bidders n varies across the auctions in the dataset. The two behavioral assumptions are:

A1: Bidders do not bid more than they are willing to pay.
A2: Bidder do not allow an opponent to win at a price they are willing to beat.

From these two assumptions, they derive bounds on the CDF of bidders' valuations $F(v)$, as a function of the CDF of bids $G(b)$ which is observed from the data.

Upper bound for $F(v)$: Obviously, from A1, $b_i \leq v_i$ implies $F(v_i) \leq G(v_i)$. They derive a tighter bound.

From Lemma 1: A1 implies that $b_{i:n} \leq v_{i:n} \Rightarrow F_{i:n}(v) \leq G_{i:n}(v)$ where $i : n$ denotes the ith highest order statistic out of n random draws.

This yields Theorem 1:

$$F(v) \le F_U(v) \equiv \min_{n,i}$$

$$\equiv \phi \in [0,1] : \quad \overbrace{\phi(G_{i:n}(v), i, n)}^{} \\ G_{i:n}(v) = \frac{n!}{(n-i)!(i-1)!} \int_0^\phi s^{i-1}(1-s)^{n-i} ds.$$

$$(6.11)$$

In the above, the function $\phi(H_{i:n}(v), i, n)$ is an "order statistic inversion" function which returns, for a given distribution of the $i : n$ order statistic $H_{i:n}(v)$, the corresponding "parent" CDF $H(v)$. $\phi(\cdot, i, n)$ is increasing in the first argument, implying that, for any i, n:

$$F(v) = \phi(F_{i:n}(v), i, n) \le \phi(G_{i:n}(v), i, n),$$

which underlies Theorem 1. Equation (6.11) is the main inequality for the upper bounds.

Lower bound: Similar calculations lead to the lower bound. From A2, we know that

$$v_i \le \begin{cases} \bar{v} & \text{if } b_i = b_{n:n}, \\ b_{n:n} + \Delta & \text{if } b_i < b_{n:n}. \end{cases}$$

In the above, $\bar{v}$ denotes the upper bound of the valuation distribution; $b_{n:n}$ denotes the maximum bid observed in an auction with n bidders, and $\Delta \ge 0$ is a known bid increment. Because Δ is known, then also $G_{n:n}^\Delta(\cdot)$, the CDF of $b_{n:n} + \Delta$, is also known.

Lemma 3. $v_{n-1:n} \le b_{n:n} + \Delta \implies F_{n-1:n}(v) \ge G_{n:n}^\Delta(v)$.

Using the same $\phi(\cdots)$ function from before, this implies that

$$F(v) = \phi(F_{n-1:n}(v), n-1, n) \ge \phi(G_{n:n}^\Delta(v), n-1, n).$$

Hence we get **Theorem 2**.

$$F(v) \ge F_L(v) \equiv \max_n \phi(G_{n:n}^\Delta(v), n-1, n). \qquad (6.12)$$

Equation (6.12) is the main inequality for the lower bound.

Bibliography

Athey, S. and P. Haile (2002): "Identification of Standard Auction Models," *Econometrica*, **70**, 2107–2140.

Guerre, E., I. Perrigne and Q. Vuong (2000): "Optimal Nonparametric Estimation of First-Price Auctions," *Econometrica*, **68**, 525–574.

Haile, P., H. Hong and M. Shum (2003): "Nonparametric Tests for Common Values in First-Price Auctions," NBER working paper #10105.

Haile, P. and E. Tamer (2003): "Inference with an Incomplete Model of English Auctions," *J. Polit. Econ.*, **111**, 1–51.

Hendricks, K., J. Pinkse and R. Porter (2003): "Empirical Implications of Equilibrium Bidding in First-Price, Symmetric, Common-Value Auctions," *Rev. Econ. Stud.*, **70**, 115–145.

Klemperer, P. (1999): "Auction Theory: A Guide to the Literature," *J. Econ. Surv.*, **13**, 227–286.

Laffont, J. J., H. Ossard and Q. Vuong (1995): "Econometrics of First-Price Auctions," *Econometrica*, **63**, 953–980.

Laffont, J. J. and Q. Vuong (1996): "Structural Analysis of Auction Data," *Am. Econ. Rev., Papers and Proceedings*, **86**, 414–420.

Li, T., I. Perrigne and Q. Vuong (2000): "Conditionally Independent Private Information in OCS Wildcat Auctions," *J. Econometrics*, **98**, 129–161.

Li, T., I. Perrigne and Q. Vuong (2002): "Structural Estimation of the Affiliated Private Value Auction Model," *RAND J. Econ.*, **33**, 171–193.

Myerson, R. (1981): "Optimal Auction Design," *Math. Oper. Res.*, **6**, 58–73.

Chapter 7

Partial Identification in Structural Models

In this set of lecture notes, we introduce the ideas related to partial identification in structural econometric models. As a motivating example, we will consider the static two-firm entry game. Despite its simplicity, it is strategically nontrivial because the entry choices of competing firms are interdependent (i.e., entry choice of firm 1 affects profits of firm 2).

As we will see, in this simple entry game, multiple equilibria are a typical problem. A literature has pointed out how, typically, the possibility of multiple equilibria in the underlying game leads to the *partial identification* of the structural model parameters.[1] This means that there are multiple values of the structural model parameters which are consistent with the observed data. Econometrically, the estimating equations in these types of settings typically take the form of "moment inequalities," and a very large literature has developed, regarding inference with moment inequalities. These lecture notes will cover these topics.

Throughout, we will employ a two-firm entry game as the running example. First, we focus on games where the moment (in)equalities are generated by "structural" errors (i.e., those observed by the firms,

---

[1]See, for instance, Tamer (2003), Ciliberto and Tamer (2009), Beresteanu, Molchanov, and Molinari (2011) and Galichon and Henry (forthcoming).

but not by the econometrician). A typical paper here is Ciliberto and Tamer's (2009) analysis of entry in airline markets. Second, we consider the case where the moment (in)equalities are generated by nonstructural, expectational errors, which are not known by agents at the time that their decisions are made. This follows the approach taken in Pakes *et al.* (2007).

7.1 Entry Games with Structural Errors

Consider a simple 2-firm entry model. Let $a_i \in \{0,1\}$ denote the action of player $i = 1, 2$. The profits are given by:

$$\Pi_i(s) = \begin{cases} \beta's - \delta a_{-i} + \epsilon_i & \text{if } a_i = 1, \\ 0 & \text{otherwise,} \end{cases}$$

s denotes market-level control variables. Entry choices are interdependent, in the sense that, firm 1's profits from entering (and, hence, decision to enter) depend on whether firm 2 is in the market.

As before, the error terms ϵ_i are assumed to be observed by both firms, but not by the econometrician. This is a "perfect information" game. We also consider "incomplete information" games below.

For fixed values of the errors $\epsilon \equiv (\epsilon_1, \epsilon_2)$ and parameters $\theta \equiv (\alpha_1, \alpha_2, \beta_1, \beta_2)$, the Nash equilibrium values a_1^*, a_2^* must satisfy best-response conditions. For fixed (θ, ϵ), the best-response conditions are:

$$\begin{aligned} a_1^* = 1 &\Leftrightarrow \Pi_1(a_2^*) \geq 0, \\ a_1^* = 0 &\Leftrightarrow \Pi_1(a_2^*) < 0, \\ a_2^* = 1 &\Leftrightarrow \Pi_2(a_1^*) \geq 0, \\ a_2^* = 0 &\Leftrightarrow \Pi_2(a_1^*) < 0. \end{aligned}$$

For some values of parameters, there may be multiple equilibria (Figure 7.1).

Given this setup, we derive the following inequalities for the probabilities of the four entry outcomes:

- $P_{10}^U(\beta, \delta) \equiv [1 - \Phi(-\beta's)][\Phi(\delta - \beta's)]$

$$\geq Pr[(1,0)|s] \geq [1 - \Phi(-\beta's)]\Phi(-\beta's)$$

$$+ [1 - \Phi(\delta - \beta's)][\Phi(\delta - \beta's) - \Phi(-\beta's)] \equiv P_{10}^L(\beta, \delta).$$

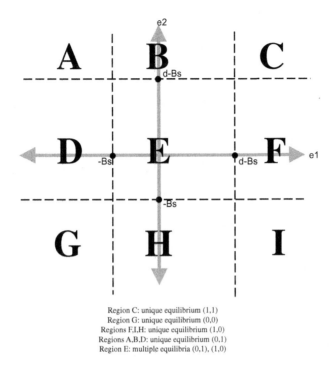

Region C: unique equilibrium (1,1)
Region G: unique equilibrium (0,0)
Regions F,I,H: unique equilibrium (1,0)
Regions A,B,D: unique equilibrium (0,1)
Region E: multiple equilibria (0,1), (1,0)

Figure 7.1: Equilibrium Regions in Two-Film Entry Game.

- $P_{01}^{U}(\beta, \delta) \equiv [1 - \Phi(-\beta' s)][\Phi(\delta - \beta' s)]$

$$\geq Pr[(0,1)|s] \geq [1 - \Phi(-\beta' s)]\Phi(-\beta' s)$$
$$+ [1 - \Phi(\delta - \beta' s)][\Phi(\delta - \beta' s) - \Phi(-\beta' s)] \equiv P_{01}^{L}(\beta, \delta).$$

- $[\Phi(-\beta' s)]^2 = Pr[(0,0)|s].$
- $[1 - \Phi(\delta - \beta' s)]^2 = Pr[(1,1)|s].$

Agnosticism, multiple equilibrium, and partial identification: a thought experiment. Why does multiple equilibria go hand-in-hand with partial identification? Consider a thought experiment, where John and Jill are given the same dataset, on entry outcomes from a two-firm entry game, played across a large number of identical markets. John and Jill agree on the model, but disagree about the equilibrium selection procedure. Let's say John believes that, when there are multiple equilibria, the $(0,1)$ outcome always obtains, so that $\Pr[(0,1)|s] = P_{01}^U$ and $\Pr[(1,0)|s] = P_{10}^L$. Jill believes, however, that in the multiple equilibria region, the two firms flip a coin so that $(0,1)$ and $(1,0)$ occur with 50–50 odds, so that $\Pr[(0,1)|s] = 0.5(P_{01}^L + P_{01}^U)$ and $\Pr[(1,0)|s] = 0.5(P_{10}^L + P_{10}^U)$.

Now they take the data and estimate the model parameters under their assumptions. (For instance, they could run maximum likelihood.) Obviously, John and Jill will obtain different estimates of the parameters (β, δ). Who is right? As an agnostic observer, you must conclude that *both* are right. Therefore, in this multiple equilibria setting, agnosticism about the equilibrium selection rule drives the partial identification of the model parameters.

7.1.1 Deriving moment inequalities

Define the mutually exclusive outcome indicators:

$$
\begin{aligned}
Y_1 &= \mathbf{1}(a_1 = 1, a_2 = 0), \\
Y_2 &= \mathbf{1}(a_1 = 0, a_2 = 1), \\
Y_3 &= \mathbf{1}(a_1 = 0, a_2 = 0), \\
Y_4 &= \mathbf{1}(a_1 = 1, a_2 = 1).
\end{aligned}
\tag{7.1}
$$

We observe a dataset $\vec{Y}_t = \{Y_{1t}, Y_{2t}, Y_{3t}, Y_{4t}\}$ for a series of markets $t = 1, \ldots, T$. From this data, we can estimate the outcome probabilities $\hat{P}_{00}, \hat{P}_{01}, \hat{P}_{10}, \hat{P}_{11}$ (we ignore market-specific covariates s for now). These estimates can be plugged into the probability inequalities above, leading to *moment inequalities* which define the identified set of parameters (β, δ).

The identified set as defined by these moment inequalities, is not "sharp": don't impose joint restrictions in inequalities. Specifically, if you are at upper bound of the first equation, you cannot be at upper bound of second equation. That is, you need to impose an additional equation on

$$
P[(0,1) \cup (1,0)|s] = P_{10}^U(\beta, \delta) + P_{01}^L(\beta, \delta) = P_{01}^U(\beta, \delta) + P_{10}^L(\beta, \delta).
$$

There are alternative ways around this multiple equilibrium problem. Instead of modeling events $Y_1 = 1$ and $Y_2 = 1$ separately, we model the aggregate event $Y_5 \equiv Y_1 + Y_2 = 1$, which is the event that *only one firm* enters. In other words, just model likelihood of *number of entrants* but not identities of entrants. Indeed, this was done in Berry's (1994) paper.

7.2　Entry Games with Expectational Errors

In contrast to the above, Pakes, Porter, Ho, and Ishii (PPHI) derive the moment inequalities directly from the optimality conditions. By allowing more general error structures, a large variety of moment inequalities can be generated. We illustrate this approach again for the two-firm entry example.

Nash equilibrium:　In the two-firm entry game, if the actions (a_1^*, a_2^*) are observed, then the inequalities for a Nash equilibrium are,

$$E\left[\pi_1(a_1^*, a_2^*, z)|\Omega_1\right] - E\left[\pi(a, a_2^*, z)|\Omega_1\right] > 0, \quad \text{for } a \neq a_1^*,$$

$$E\left[\pi_2(a_1^*, a_2^*, z)|\Omega_2\right] - E\left[\pi(a_1^*, a, z)|\Omega_2\right] > 0, \quad \text{for } a \neq a_2^*. \quad (7.2)$$

These conditions are from the optimizing firms' point of view, so in order for the expectations above to be nontrivial, implicitly there are some variables in z, which are not observed by the firms (i.e., not in the information sets Ω_1, or Ω_2).

Accordingly, PPHI parameterize (for all i, a_1, and a_2)

$$\pi_i(a_1, a_2, z) = r_i(a_1, a_2, z; \theta).$$

In the above, $r_i(a_1, a_2, z; \theta)$ is a particular functional form for firm i's counterfactual profits under action profile (a_1, a_2), which is assumed to be known by researchers, up to the unknown parameters θ.[2]

Hence, plugging into the equilibrium inequalities, we have the conditional moment inequalities which we can use to estimate θ:

$$E\left[r_1(a_1^*, a_2^*, z; \theta)|\Omega_1\right] - E\left[r_1(a, a_2^*, z; \theta)|\Omega_1\right] > 0, \quad \text{for } a \neq a_1^*,$$

$$E\left[r_2(a_1^*, a_2^*, z; \theta)|\Omega_2\right] - E\left[r_2(a_1^*, a, z; \theta)|\Omega_2\right] > 0, \quad \text{for } a \neq a_2^*.$$

$$(7.3)$$

---

[2]We can relax this to allow for $\pi_i(a_1, a_2, z) = r_i(a_1, a_2, z; \theta) + v_{i,a_1,a_2}$, where $v_{...}$ are errors which have mean zero conditional on Ω_i.

To operationalize this, consider some instruments $Z_{1i}, \ldots,$ $Z_{Mi} \in \Omega_i$, and transform them such that they are nonnegative-valued. Then, the conditional moment inequalities above imply the unconditional inequalities

$$E\left[(r_1(a_1^*, a_2^*, z; \theta) - r_1(a, a_2^*, z; \theta)) * Z_m\right] > 0,$$

$$\text{for } a \neq a_1^*, \ m = 1, \ldots, M,$$

$$E\left[(r_2(a_1^*, a_2^*, z; \theta) - r_2(a_1^*, a, z; \theta)) * Z_m\right] > 0,$$

$$\text{for } a \neq a_2^*, \ m = 1, \ldots, M. \qquad (7.4)$$

Accordingly, these unconditional moments can be estimated by sample averages.

7.3   Inference Procedures with Moment Inequalities/Incomplete Models

In cases when a model is not sufficient to point-identify a parameter θ, goal of estimation is to recover the "identified set": the set of θ's (call this Θ_0) which satisfy population analogs of moment inequalities $Eg(x, \theta) \geq 0$:

$$\Theta_0 = \{\theta : \ Eg(x, \theta) \geq 0\}.$$

With small samples, we will never know Θ_0 exactly.

7.3.1   Identified parameter vs. identified set

The existing literature stresses two approaches for inference in partially identified models: deriving confidence sets with either cover the (i) identified set or (ii) the elements in the identified set with some prescribed probability. More formally, a given confidence set $\hat{\Theta}_n$ satisfies either of the asymptotic conditions,

$$\text{(i)} \quad \liminf_{n\to\infty} P(\Theta_0 \subset \hat{\Theta}_n) = 1 - \alpha \quad \text{or}$$

$$\text{(ii)} \quad \liminf_{n\to\infty} \inf_{\theta \in \Theta_0} P(\theta \in \hat{\Theta}_n) = 1 - \alpha,$$

where $1 - \alpha$ denotes a prescribed coverage probability.

This distinction was emphasized by Imbens and Manski (2004). Generally, CS for "identified parameter" will be smaller than *CS* for "identified set." Intuition: consider identified interval $\theta \in [a, b]$ with estimators $\hat{a}_n$ and $\hat{b}_n$. For asymptotic normal estimates, we can form the symmetric two-sided $1 - \alpha$ confidence interval as $[\underline{a}_n, \bar{a}_n] = \hat{a}_n \pm z_{\alpha/2}\sigma/\sqrt{n}$, where $z_{1-\alpha/2}$ denotes $(1-\alpha/2)$th quantile of $N(0, 1)$; analogously for $[\underline{b}_n, \bar{b}_n]$.

Consider the intuitive confidence region $\mathcal{C}_n \equiv [\underline{a}_n, \bar{b}_n]$. This should cover identified interval $[a, b]$ with asymptotic probability $(1 - \alpha)$, for the usual reasons.

But consider coverage probability of $\mathcal{C}_n$ for any point $\theta \in [a, b]$. As $n \to \infty$, any $\theta \in (a, b)$ will lie in $\mathcal{C}$ with probability 1. For $\theta = a$: note that by construction, $[\underline{a}_n, \bar{a}_n]$ covers a with asymptotic probability $(1 - \alpha)$, so that $\mathcal{C}_n \supset [\underline{a}_n, \bar{a}_n]$ covers a with probability $\geq (1 - \alpha)$ asymptotically. Similarly with $\theta = b$. Indeed, for this case, Imbens and Manski show that the "doubly one-sided interval" $[\hat{a}_n - z_{1-\alpha}\sigma/\sqrt{n}, \hat{b}_n + z_{1-\alpha}\sigma/\sqrt{n}]$ covers each $\theta \in [a, b]$ with asymptotic probability no smaller than $(1 - \alpha)$.

7.3.2 Confidence sets which cover "identified parameters"

In constructing confidence intervals of the form (ii); i.e., those which cover each identified parameter with some prescribed probability, we utilize the traditional approach to confidence set construction: we "invert" test of the point hypotheses $H_0 : \theta \in \Theta_0 \Leftrightarrow Eg(x, \theta) \geq 0$ vs. $H_1 : \theta \notin \Theta_0$. Different confidence sets arise from using different test statistics (Wald-type statistics, empirical likelihood statistics, etc.) For a given test statistic, let the critical value $c_{1-\alpha}(\theta)$ denote the (asymptotic) $1 - \alpha$ quantile, under the null. Then we form our confidence set:

$$\hat{\Theta}_n = \{\theta : T_n(\theta) \leq c_{1-\alpha}(\theta)\}, \tag{7.5}$$

where $T_n(\theta)$ denotes the sample test statistic, evaluated at the parameter θ.

As an example of such an approach, consider the moment inequalities $Eg(x; \theta) \leq 0$, where $g(\cdots)$ is a M-dimensional moment vector with typical element $g^m(x; \theta)$. These moments can be approximated by the sample averages $Eg(x; \theta) \approx \frac{1}{T} \sum_{t=1}^{T} g(x_t; \theta) \equiv g_T(\theta)$. Then we consider the quadratic form:

$$Q_T(\theta; W) = T \cdot \sum_{m=1}^{M} [g_T^m(\theta)/\sigma_T^m(\theta)]_+^2, \qquad (7.6)$$

where $\sigma_T^m(\theta)$ is an estimate of the standard error of the sample moment $g_T^m(\theta)$, and $[z]_+ \equiv z \cdot \mathbf{1}(z > 0)$ is the amount that a given sample moment violates the inequality. Now, for each θ, we consider testing the hypothesis

$$H_\theta : \; Eg(x; \theta) \leq 0 \Leftrightarrow \theta \in \Theta_0.$$

Note that if these were moment *equalities* $(Eg(x; \theta) = 0)$, then the analogous test statistic which we would use here would be $T \cdot \sum_{m=1}^{M} [g_T^m(\theta)/\sigma_T^m(\theta)]^2$, which is just the usual quadratic form GMM test statistic. Typically, in this case, $Q_T(\theta)$ tends to a χ^2 distribution under the (moment equality) null, and accordingly we can obtain the critical value $c_{1-\alpha}$ (which will typically be the same for all values of θ).

However, in the case of moment inequalities, the asymptotic distribution of $Q_T(\theta)$ will not take a convenient closed form, and it may also vary with the particular parameter value θ.[3] In short, the reason for this is that the asymptotic distribution of $Q_T(\theta)$ depends on which of the moment inequalities are binding (i.e., which of them are exactly $Eg_m(x; \theta) = 0$); and the set of moment inequalities which are binding may vary depending on θ.[4]

For this reason, for each value of θ, the critical values $c_{1-\alpha}(\theta)$ for these tests are typically approximated via data resampling

---

[3]See Wolak (1989) for early work on deriving these nonstandard distributions.
[4]See Andrews and Soares (2010). There is a large and active econometrics literature on inference with moment inequalities, including Chernozhukov, Hong, and Tamer (2007), Canay (2010), Andrews, Berry, and Jia (2004), etc.

procedures (such as bootstrap or subsampling), in order to obtain the confidence set (7.5).

7.3.3 Confidence sets which cover the identified set

We discuss here the estimation procedure of Romano and Shaikh (2010). Roughly speaking, just as confidence sets which cover an identified parameter are obtained by inverting tests for a null hypothesis involving a single value of θ, a confidence set which has nice coverage properties for the whole identified set Θ_0 is obtained by inverting a *multiple hypothesis test* for a family of null hypotheses involving a *set* of values of θ.

Let P denote true (but unknown) data-generating process of data, and let Θ denote the parameter space. Define identified set as:

$$\Theta_0(P) \equiv \text{argmin}_{\theta \in \Theta} Q(\theta, P) \Leftrightarrow \{\theta \in \Theta : \ Q(\theta, P) = 0\}.$$

Let $Q_n(\theta)$ denote the sample objective function, and a_n a rate of convergence such that as $n \to \infty$, $a_n \to \infty$ and $a_n Q_n(\theta) \xrightarrow{d} \mathcal{L}(\theta)$, a nondegenerate limiting distribution.

For the case of inequality constrained moment conditions $E_P g_m$ $(Y, \theta) \leq 0$, for m indexing the moment conditions, one possibility is to define a least-squares objective function $Q(\theta, P) = \sum_m [E_p g_m(Y, \theta)]_+^2$ with small-sample analog $Q_n(\theta) = \sum_m [\frac{1}{T} g_m(Y_t, \theta)]_+^2$.

The notation $[y]_+$ is shorthand for $y \cdot \mathbf{1}(y > 0)$. For the specific case of the first inequality in the conditions above, $g(Y_t, \theta) = Y_{t1} - [1 - \Phi(-\beta's)][\Phi(\delta - \beta's)]$.

Goal of estimation: recover confidence set C_n s.t.

$$\liminf_{n \to \infty} P\{C_n \supseteq \Theta_0(P)\} = 1 - \alpha, \tag{7.7}$$

for some level α.

Romano–Shaikh show:

- This estimation problem is equivalent to a testing problem, where the goal is to test the family (continuum) of hypotheses,

$$H_\theta : \ \theta \in \Theta_0(P), \ \forall \ \theta \in \Theta,$$

subject to a restriction on the "family-wise error rate" FWER such that

$$\limsup_{n\to\infty} \text{FWER}_{P,n} = \alpha, \tag{7.8}$$

where,

$$\text{FWER}_{P,n} = P\{\text{with } n \text{ obs., reject at least 1 "true"}$$
$$\text{null hypothesis } H_\theta \text{ s.t. } Q(\theta, P) = 0\}.$$

FWER is a generalization of type I error (when you have unidimensional hypothesis test).
This does not define the test statistic, just a characteristic that the test should satisfy.

- Note that

$$1 - \text{FWER}_{P,n} = P\{\text{with } n \text{ obs., reject no null hypothesis}$$
$$H_\theta \text{ s.t. } Q(\theta, P) = 0\}$$
$$= P\{\Theta_0(P) \subseteq C_n\}. \tag{7.9}$$

Hence the FWER restriction (7.8) is equivalent to,

$$\limsup_{n\to\infty} 1 - P\{\Theta_0(P) \subseteq C_n\} = \alpha$$
$$\Leftrightarrow \liminf_{n\to\infty} P\{\Theta_0(P) \subseteq C_n\} = 1 - \alpha, \tag{7.10}$$

which is the required criterion (7.7).

- The following "stepdown" algorithm yields, at the end, a set C_n satisfying Eq. (7.7).

1. Start with $S^1 = \Theta$ (the entire parameter space).
2. Evaluate this test statistic:

$$\tau_n(S^1, \theta) \equiv \max_{\theta \in S^1} a_n Q_n(\theta).$$

3. Compare test statistic $\tau_n(S^1, \theta)$ to critical value $c_n(S^1, 1 - \alpha)$, where critical value is obtained by subsampling:

    — Consider subsamples of size b_n from original dataset. There are $N_n \equiv \binom{n}{b_n}$ subsampled datasets from the original dataset, indexed by $i = 1, \ldots, N_n$ (as $n \to \infty$, $\frac{b_n}{n} \to 0$).

— For each subsampled dataset i: compute the subsampled test statistic

$$\kappa_{i,n}(S^1, \theta) \equiv \max_{\theta \in S^1} a_b Q_b(\theta).$$

— Set $c_n(S^1, 1-\alpha)$ to $(1-\alpha)$th quantile amongst $\{\kappa_{1,n}(S^1, \theta), \ldots, \kappa_{N_n,n}(S^1, \theta)\}$.

4. If $\tau_n(S^1, \theta) \leq c_n(S^1, 1 - \alpha)$, then stop, and set $C_n = S^1$,
5. If $\tau_n(S^1, \theta) > c_n(S^1, 1 - \alpha)$, then set

$$S^2 = \{\theta \in S^1 : a_n Q_n(\theta) \leq c_n(S^1, 1 - \alpha)\}.$$

Repeat from step 2, using S^2 in place of S^1.

7.4 Random Set Approach

- Beresteanu and Molinari (2008) and Beresteanu, Molchanov, and Molinari (2011).
- Probability space $(\Omega, \mathcal{A}, \mu)$.
- Set-valued random variable ("random set" for short) $F : \Omega \mapsto K(\mathbb{R}^d)$, where $K(\mathbb{R}^d)$ denotes the set of nonempty closed subsets in $\mathbb{R}^d$.
- Inner product $\langle \cdot, \cdot \rangle$ in $\mathbb{R}^d$ is vector dot product; Euclidean distance between $\vec{a}, \vec{b} \in \mathbb{R}^d$ is $||\vec{a} - \vec{b}|| = \sqrt{\langle \vec{a} - \vec{b}, \vec{a} - \vec{b} \rangle}$.
- $K(\mathbb{R}^d)$ is metric space with Hausdorff distance:

$$H(A, B) = \max(d_H(A, B), d_H(B, A)), \quad d_H(A, B)$$
$$= \sup_{\vec{a} \in A} \inf_{\vec{b} \in B} ||\vec{a} - \vec{b}||.$$

- Selection of random set F is random vector $\vec{f} : \Omega \mapsto \mathbb{R}^d$ such that $\vec{f}(\omega) \in F(\omega)$. $S(F)$ is set of selections of F.
- Aumann expectation: $\mathbb{E}(F) = \left\{\int_\Omega \vec{f} d\mu, \ \vec{f} \in S(F)\right\}$.

  Note: for given $\vec{f}$, $\int_\Omega \vec{f} d\mu$ is d-dim. vector with i-th element $\int_\Omega f_i(\omega)\mu(d\omega)$.
- Support function for a set $R \in K(\mathbb{R}^d)$ is $s(\vec{p}, R) = \sup_{\vec{r} \in R} \langle \vec{p}, \vec{r} \rangle$, for all $\vec{p} \in \mathbb{R}^d$. Support function for a set R is the *Fenchel/Legendre transform* of the indicator function for that set,

defined as $\delta_R(\vec{p}) = 0 \cdot \mathbf{1}(\vec{p} \in R) + (+\infty) \cdot \mathbf{1}(\vec{p} \notin R).$[5] In this sense, the support function is an equivalent representation of the set R.

7.4.1 Application: Sharp identified region for games with multiple equilibria

- Outcome space $\mathcal{Y} \subset \mathbb{R}^k$; randomness indexes by $\omega \in \Omega$ with probability P.
- Random set $Q(\omega; \theta) \subset \mathcal{Y}$, for all $\omega \in \Omega$: for each ω, the realization of the random set $Q(\omega; \theta)$ is the set (possibly singleton) of outcomes which could occur in an equilibrium of the game, given (ω, θ).
- Aumann expectation $\mathbb{E}Q(\omega; \theta) \subset \mathcal{Y}$: set of expected outcomes consistent with some equlibrium selection rule.
- Average outcomes observed in data: $E(y)$, for $y \in \mathcal{Y}$.
- Sharp identified region:

$$\Theta_0 = \{\theta : E(y) \in \mathbb{E}Q(\omega; \theta)\},$$

which is typically a convex set. Using support function $s(u, \mathbb{E}Q(\omega; \theta))$, we can equivalently denote this by (this is the *separating hyperlane theorem!*),

$$
\begin{aligned}
\Theta_0 &= \{\theta : E(y) \in \mathbb{E}Q(\omega; \theta)\} \\
&= \left\{\theta : u'E(y) \leq s(u, \mathbb{E}Q(\omega; \theta)), \ \forall u \in \mathbb{R}^k, ||u|| = 1\right\} \\
&= \left\{\theta : u'E(y) \leq Es(u, Q(\omega; \theta)), \ \forall u \in \mathbb{R}^k, ||u|| = 1\right\} \\
&= \left\{\theta : \max_{u \in \mathbb{R}^k, ||u||=1} \left[u'E(y) - Es(u, Q(\omega; \theta))\right] \leq 0\right\},
\end{aligned}
$$

which, for each θ, is a k-dimensional optimization program. The final equality in the above display uses the random set result that

$$s(u, \mathbb{E}Q(\omega; \theta)) = Es(u, Q(\omega; \theta)).$$

---

[5]By definition of the Fenchel transform (cf. Borwein and Lewis, 2006, p. 55), the Fenchel conjugate of $\delta_R(\vec{p})$ is the function $\delta_R^*(\vec{p}) \equiv \sup_{\vec{r} \in R} \{\langle \vec{p}, \vec{r} \rangle - \delta_R(r)\} = \sup_{\vec{r} \in R} \{\langle \vec{p}, \vec{r} \rangle\} = s(\vec{p}, R).$

Bibliography

Andrews, D., S. Berry and P. Jia (2004): "Confidence Regions for Parameters in Discrete Games with Multiple Equilibria, with an Application to Discount Chain Store Location," mimeo, Yale University.

Andrews, D. W. K. and G. Soares (2010): "Inference for Parameters Defined by Moment Inequalities Using Generalized Moment Selection," *Econometrica*, **78**, 119–157.

Beresteanu, A. and F. Molinari (2008): "Asymptotic Properties for a Class of Partially Identified Models," *Econometrica*, **76**, 763–814.

Beresteanu, A., I. Molchanov and F. Molinari (2011): "Sharp Identification Regions in Models With Convex Moment Predictions," *Econometrica*, **79**, 1785–1821.

Borwein, J. and A. Lewis (2006): *Convex Analysis and Nonlinear Optimization*. Springer Verlag.

Canay, I. A. (2010): "EL Inference for Partially Identified Models: Large Deviations Optimality and Bootstrap Validity," *J. Econometrics*, **156**, 408–425.

Chernozhukov, V., H. Hong and E. Tamer (2007): "Estimation and confidence regions for parameter sets in econometric models," *Econometrica*, **75**, 1234–1275.

Ciliberto, F. and E. Tamer (2009): "Market Structure and Multiple Equilibria in Airline Markets," *Econometrica*, **77**, 1791–1828.

Galichon, A. and M. Henry (forthcoming): "Inference in models with multiple equilibria," *Rev. Econ. Stud.*

Ho, K., J. Ho and J. Mortimer (2012): "The Use of Full-Line Forcing Contracts in the Video Rental Industry," *Am. Econ. Rev.*

Imbens, G. and C. F. Manski (2004): "Confidence Intervals for Partially Identified Parameters," *Econometrica*, **72**, 1845–1857.

Pakes, A., J. Porter, K. Ho and J. Ishii (2007): "Moment Inequalities and their Application," Manuscript, Harvard University.

Romano, J. and A. Shaikh (2010): "Inference for the Identified Set in Partially Identified Econometric Models," *Econometrica*, **78**, 169–211.

Tamer, E. (2003): "Incomplete simultaneous discrete response model with multiple equilibria," *Rev. Econ. Stud.*, **70**, 147–165.

Wolak, F. (1989): "Local and Global Testing of Linear and Nonlinear Inequality Constraints in Nonlinear Econometric Models," *Econometric Theory*, **1**, 1–35.

Chapter 8

Background: Simulation Methods

Simulation methods have played a very important role in econometrics. The main principle of integration via simulation ("Monte Carlo integration") is the following:

Approximate an expectation as a sample average.

The validity of this principle is ensured by law of large numbers. Let $x^1, x^2, \ldots, x^S$ be S identically and independently distributed (i.i.d.) draws from some distribution with density $f(X)$. Then

$$EX = \int x f(x) dx \approx \frac{1}{S} \sum_{s=1}^{S} x^s.$$

Simulation can be a very useful tool for computing integrals, because most integrals can be written as an expectation. To simulate from a distribution with CDF F, exploit quantile transform:

- Draw $Z \sim U[0,1]$.
- Transform $X = F^{-1}(Z)$. Then $X \sim F$.

Here, we consider several interesting applications of the simulation approach in econometrics.

8.1   Importance Sampling

Importance sampling is a more efficient approach to simulation. In essence, you take draws from an alternative distribution whose support is concentrated in the truncation region. Principle of importance sampling:

$$\int_{\mathcal{F}} s f(s) ds = \int_{\mathcal{G}} s \frac{f(s)}{g(s)} g(s) ds.$$

That is, sampling s from $f(s)$ distribution equivalent to sampling $s * w(s)$ from $g(s)$ distribution, with importance sampling weight $w(s) \equiv \frac{f(s)}{g(s)}$ (f and g should have the same support).

Simple example: You want to simulate the mean of a standard normal distribution, truncated to the unit interval [0,1]. The desired sampling density is:

$$f(x) = \frac{\phi(x)}{\int_0^1 \phi(x) dx},$$

where $\phi()$ denotes the standard normal density.

Brute force simulation: take draws x^s from $N(0, 1)$, and only keep draws in [0,1]. Simulated mean is calculated as: $\frac{\sum_{s=1}^{S} x^s \cdot \mathbf{1}(x^s \in [0,1])}{\sum_{s=1}^{S} \mathbf{1}(x^s \in [0,1])}$. Inefficient if $\sum_{s=1}^{S} \mathbf{1}(x^s \in [0,1]) \ll S$.

Importance sampling: draw from U[0,1], so that $g(x) = 1$ for $x \in [0, 1]$. For each draw, importance weight is $w^s = f(x^s) = \frac{\phi(x^s)}{\int_0^1 \phi(z) dz}$. Simulated mean is $\frac{1}{S} \sum_{s=1}^{S} x^s w^s$. Don't need to reject any draws.

8.1.1   GHK simulator: Get draws from truncated multivariate normal (MVN) distribution

You can draw from,

$$\begin{pmatrix} x_1 \\ x_2 \\ \vdots \\ x_n \end{pmatrix} \sim TN\left(\vec{\mu}, \Sigma; \vec{a}, \vec{b}\right) \equiv N\left(\vec{\mu}, \Sigma\right) \text{ s.t. } \vec{a} < \vec{x} < \vec{b}, \qquad (8.1)$$

where the difficulty is that Σ is not necessarily diagonal (i.e., elements of $\vec{x}$ are correlated).

The most obvious "brute-force" approach to simulation is an acceptance–rejection procedure, where you take draws from $N(\vec{\mu}, \Sigma)$ (the untruncated distribution), but reject all the draws which lie outside the desired truncation region. If the region is small, this procedure can be very inefficient, in the sense that you might end up rejecting very many draws.

Importance sampling from truncated MVN: Let $(u_1, \ldots, u_n)'$ denote an n-vector of independent multivariate standard normal random variables. Let $\Sigma^{1/2}$ denote the (lower-triangular) Cholesky factorization of Σ, with elements

$$
\begin{bmatrix}
s_{11} & 0 & \cdots & 0 & 0 \\
s_{21} & s_{22} & \cdots & 0 & 0 \\
\vdots & \vdots & s_{ii} & 0 & 0 \\
s_{n1} & s_{n2} & \cdots & s_{nn-1} & s_{nn}
\end{bmatrix}. \tag{8.2}
$$

Then we can rewrite (8.1) as:

$$\vec{x} = \vec{\mu} + \Sigma^{1/2}\vec{u} \sim N(\vec{\mu}, \Sigma) \text{ s.t.}$$

$$
\begin{pmatrix}
\dfrac{a_1 - \mu_1}{s_{11}} \\[2ex]
\dfrac{a_2 - \mu_2 - s_{21}u_1}{s_{22}} \\[1ex]
\vdots \\[1ex]
\dfrac{a_n - \mu_n - \sum_{i-1}^{n-1} s_{ni}u_i}{s_{nn}}
\end{pmatrix}
<
\begin{pmatrix}
u_1 \\ u_2 \\ \vdots \\ u_n
\end{pmatrix}
<
\begin{pmatrix}
\dfrac{b_1 - \mu_1}{s_{11}} \\[2ex]
\dfrac{b_2 - \mu_2 - s_{21}u_1}{s_{22}} \\[1ex]
\vdots \\[1ex]
\dfrac{b_n - \mu_n - \sum_{i-1}^{n-1} s_{ni}u_i}{s_{nn}}
\end{pmatrix}.
$$

$$\tag{8.3}$$

The above suggests that the answer is to draw $(u_1, \ldots, u_n)$ **recursively.** First draw u_1^s from $N(0, 1; \frac{a_1 - \mu_1}{s_{11}}, \frac{b_1 - \mu_1}{s_{11}})$, then u_2^s from $N(0, 1; \frac{a_2 - \mu_2 - s_{21}u_1^s}{s_{22}}, \frac{b_2 - \mu_2 - s_{21}u_1^s}{s_{22}})$, and so on.

Finally we can transform $(u_1^s, \ldots, u_n^s)$ to the desired $(x_1^s, \ldots, x_n^s)$ via the transformation

$$\vec{x}^s = \vec{\mu} + \Sigma^{1/2} \vec{u}^s. \tag{8.4}$$

Remark 1. It is easy to draw an n-dimensional vector $\vec{u}$ of independent truncated standard normal random variables with rectangular truncation conditions: $\vec{c} < \vec{u} < \vec{d}$. You draw a vector of independent uniform variables $\vec{\tilde{u}} \sim \mathcal{U}[\Phi(\vec{c}), \Phi(\vec{d})]$[1] and then transform $u_i = \Phi^{-1}(\tilde{u}_i)$.

Remark 2. The GHK simulator is an importance sampler. The importance sampling density is the MVN density $N(\vec{\mu}, \Sigma)$ truncated to the region characterized in Eq. (8.3). This is a recursively characterized truncation region, in that the range of, say, x_3 depends on the draw of x_1 and x_2. Note that truncation region is different for each draw. This is different than the MVN density $N(\vec{\mu}, \Sigma)$ truncated to the region $(\vec{a} \leq \vec{x} \leq \vec{b})$.[2]

For the GHK simulator, the truncation probability for each draw $\vec{x}^s$ is given by:

$$\tau^s \equiv \left[\Phi\left(\frac{b_1 - \mu_1}{s_{11}}\right) - \Phi\left(\frac{a_1 - \mu_1}{s_{11}}\right) \right] \prod_{i=2}^{m} \left[\Phi\left(\frac{b_i - \mu_i - \sum_{j=1}^{i-1} s_{ij} u_j^s}{s_{ii}}\right) \right.$$

$$\left. - \Phi\left(\frac{a_i - \mu_i - \sum_{j=1}^{i-1} s_{ij} u_j^s}{s_{ii}}\right) \right]. \tag{8.5}$$

Remark 3. τ^s (even just for one draw: cf. Gourieroux and Monfort, 1996, p. 99) is an unbiased estimator of the truncation probability $\text{Prob}(\vec{a} < \vec{x} < \vec{b})$. But in general, we can get a more precise estimate by averaging over w^s:

$$T_{\vec{a},\vec{b}} \equiv \text{Prob}(\vec{a} < \vec{x} < \vec{b}) \approx \frac{1}{S} \sum_s \tau^s, \tag{8.6}$$

for (say) S simulation draws.

---

[1] Just draw $\hat{u}$ from $\mathcal{U}[0,1]$ and transform $\tilde{u} = \Phi(c) + (\Phi(d) - \Phi(c))\hat{u}$.
[2] See Hajivassiliou and Ruud (1994, p. 2,005).

Hence, the importance sampling weight for each GHK draw is the ratio of the GHK truncation probability to the original desired truncation probability: $w^s \equiv \tau^s / T_{\vec{a},\vec{b}} \approx \tau^s / \frac{1}{S} \sum_s \tau^s$.

Hence, the GHK simulator for $\int_{\vec{a} \leq \vec{x} \leq \vec{b}} \vec{x} f(\vec{x}) d\vec{x}$, where $f(\vec{x})$ denote the $N(\vec{\mu}, \Sigma)$ density, is $\frac{1}{S} \sum_{s=1}^{S} \vec{x}^s w(x^s)$, or $\sum_s \vec{x}^s \tau^s / \sum_s \tau^s$.

8.1.2 Monte Carlo integration using the GHK simulator

Clearly, if we can get draws from truncated multivariate distributions using the GHK simulator, we can use these draws to calculate integrals of functions of $\vec{x}$. There are two important cases here, which it is crucial not to confuse.

Integrating over untruncated distribution F(x̃), but ã < x̃ < b̃ defines region of integration.

If we want to calculate

$$\int_{\vec{a} < \vec{x} < \vec{b}} g(\vec{x}) f(\vec{x}) d\vec{x}, \qquad (8.7)$$

where f denotes the $N(\vec{\mu}, \Sigma)$ density, we can use the GHK draws to derive a Monte Carlo estimate:

$$E_{\vec{a} < \vec{x} < \vec{b}} g(\vec{x}) \approx \frac{1}{S} \sum_s g(\vec{x}^s) * \tau^s. \qquad (8.8)$$

Here the weight is just τ^s (not w^s), because the desired sampling distribution is the *untruncated* MVN density. The most widely-cited example of this is the likelihood function for the multinomial probit model (cf. McFadden, 1989).

Multinomial probit with K choices, and utility from choice k $U_k = X\beta_k + \epsilon_k$. Probability that choice k is chosen is probability that $\nu_i \equiv \epsilon_i - \epsilon_k < X\beta_i - X\beta_k$, for all $i \neq k$. For each parameter vector β, use GHK to draw S $(K-1)$-dimensional vectors $\vec{\nu}^s$ subject to $\vec{\nu} < (x\vec{\beta})$. Likelihood function is

$$\text{Prob}(k) = \int_{\vec{\nu}} \mathbf{1}\left(\vec{\nu} < (x\vec{\beta})\right) f(\vec{\nu}) d\vec{\nu}$$

$$= \int_{\vec{\nu} < (x\vec{\beta})} f(\vec{\nu}) d\vec{\nu}$$

$$\approx \frac{1}{S} \sum_s \tau^s. \tag{8.9}$$

8.1.3 Integrating over truncated (conditional) distribution $F(\vec{x}|\vec{a} < \vec{x} < \vec{b})$

The most common case of this is calculating conditional expectations (note that the multinomial probit choice probability is *not* a conditional probability!).[3]

If we want to calculate

$$E_{\vec{a}<\vec{x}<\vec{b}} g(\vec{x}) = \int_{\vec{a}<\vec{x}<\vec{b}} g(\vec{x}) f(\vec{x}|\vec{a} < \vec{x} < \vec{b}) d\vec{x} = \frac{\int_{\vec{a}<\vec{x}<\vec{b}} g(\vec{x}) f(\vec{x}) d\vec{x}}{\text{Prob}(\vec{a} < \vec{x} < \vec{b})}. \tag{8.10}$$

As before, we can use the GHK draws to derive a Monte Carlo estimate:

$$E_{\vec{a}<\vec{x}<\vec{b}} g(\vec{x}) \approx \frac{1}{T_{\vec{a},\vec{b}}} \frac{1}{S} \sum_s g(\vec{x}^s) * \tau^s. \tag{8.11}$$

The crucial difference between this case and the previous one is that we integrate over a conditional distribution by essentially integrating over the unconditional distribution over the restricted support, but then we need to divide through by the probability of the conditioning event (i.e., the truncation probability).

---

[3]This is a crucial point. The conditional probability of choice k conditional on choice k is trivially 1!

An example of this comes from structural common-value auction models, where:

$$v(x, x) \equiv \mathcal{E}\left(v|x_1 = x, \min_{j \neq 1} x_j = x\right)$$

$$= \underbrace{\int \cdots \int}_{x_k \geq x,\ \forall k=3,\dots,n} \mathcal{E}(v|x_1, \dots, x_n)$$

$$\times\, dF(x_3, \dots, x_n|x_1 = x, x_2 = x, x_k \geq x, k = 3, \dots, n; \theta)$$

$$= \frac{1}{T_x} \underbrace{\int \cdots \int}_{x_k \geq x,\ \forall k=3,\dots,n} \mathcal{E}(v|x_1, \dots, x_n)$$

$$\times\, dF(x_3, \dots, x_n|x_1 = x, x_2 = x; \theta), \qquad (8.12)$$

where F here denotes the conditional distribution of the signals $x_3, \dots, x_n$, conditional on $x_1 = x_2 = x$, and T_x denotes the probability that $(x_k \geq x, k = 3, \dots, n|x_1 = x, x_2 = x; \theta)$.

If we assume that $\vec{x} \equiv (x_1, \dots, x_n)'$ are jointly log-normal, it turns out we can use the GHK simulator to get draws of $\tilde{x} \equiv \log \vec{x}$ from a MVN distribution subject to the truncation conditions $\tilde{x}_1 = \tilde{x}, \tilde{x}_2 = \tilde{x}, \tilde{x}_j \geq \tilde{x}, \forall j = 3, \dots, n$. Let $\mathcal{A}(x)$ denote the truncation region, for each given x.

Then we approximate:

$$v(x, x) \approx \frac{1}{T_{\mathcal{A}(x)}} \frac{1}{S} \sum_s \mathcal{E}(v|\tilde{x}^s) * \tau^s, \qquad (8.13)$$

where $T_{\mathcal{A}(x)}$ is approximated by $\frac{1}{S} \sum_s \tau^s$.

8.2 Markov Chain Monte Carlo (MCMC) Simulation

Source: Chib and Greenberg (1995).

8.2.1   Background: First-order Markov chains

- Random sequence $X_1, X_2, \ldots, X_n, X_{n+1}, \ldots$
- First-order Markov: $P(X_{n+1}|X_n, X_{n-1}, X_{n-2}, \ldots) = P(X_{n+1}| X_t) = P(X'|X)$. History-less. Denote this transition distribution as $P(x, dy) = Pr(X' \in dy | X = x)$.
- Invariant distribution: Π is distribution, π is density

$$\Pi(dy) = \int P(x, dy)\pi(x)dx.$$

- Markov chain converges to invariant distribution: for starting value x, we have

$$p^{(1)}(x, A) = P(x, A),$$

$$p^{(2)}(x, A) = \int_y P^{(1)}(x, dy)P(y, A),$$

$$p^{(3)}(x, A) = \int_y P^{(2)}(x, dy)P(y, A),$$

$$\cdots \cdots$$

$$p^{(n)}(x, A) = \int P^{(n-1)}(x, dy)P(y, A) \approx \Pi(A).$$

That is, for n large enough, each realization of X_n drawn according to $P(x, dy)$ is drawn from the marginal distribution $\Pi(dy)$. (Initial value x does not matter.)

- Markov chain theory is mainly concerned about: for a given kernal $P(x, dy)$, what is invariant distribution Π?
- MCMC simulation goes backwards: given a marginal distribution Π, can we create a Markov process with some kernel function, such that Π is the invariant distribution?
- Let $p(x, y)$ denote density function corresponding to kernel function $P(x, dy)$ (i.e., $P(x, A) = \int_A p(x, y)dy$). For a given π, if the following relationship is satisfied, then the kernel $P(x, dy)$ achieves π as the invariant distribution:

$$\pi(x)p(x, y) = \pi(y)p(y, x). \tag{8.14}$$

This is a "reversibility" condition: interpreting $X = x$ and $X' = y$, it (roughly) implies that the probability of transitioning from x to y is the same as transitioning from y to x.

(Note that in the strange case where $f_{X'|X} = f_{X|X'}$, then both sides of Eq. (8.14) represent two alternative ways of writing the joint density of $f_{X',X}$.)

Then π is the invariance density of $P(x, dy)$:

$$
\begin{aligned}
\int P(x, A)\pi(x)dx &= \iint_A p(x, y)dy\pi(x)dx \\
&= \int_A \int p(x, y)\pi(x)dxdy \\
&= \int_A \int p(y, x)\pi(y)dxdy \\
&= \int_A \left[\int p(y, x)dx \right] \pi(y)dy \\
&= \int_A \pi(y)dy = \Pi(A).
\end{aligned}
$$

- Can we find such a magic function $p(x, y)$ which satisfies (8.14)?
- Consider any conditional density function $q(x, y)$. Suppose that

$$
\pi(x)q(x, y) > \pi(y)q(y, x),
$$

so condition (8.14) fails. We will "fudge" $q(x, y)$ so that (8.14) holds.

8.2.2 Metropolis–Hastings approach

- Introduce the "fudge factor" $\alpha(x, y) \leq 1$, such that

$$
\pi(x)q(x, y)\alpha(x, y) = \pi(y)q(y, x)\alpha(y, x).
$$

When Eq. (8.14) is violated such that LHS>RHS, you want to set $\alpha(x, y) < 1$ but $\alpha(y, x) = 1$. Vice versa, if LHS<RHS, then you

want $\alpha(x, y) = 1$ but $\alpha(y, x) < 1$. We can summarize this as:

$$\alpha(x, y) = \min\left[\frac{\pi(y)q(y, x)}{\pi(x)q(x, y)}, 1\right]. \qquad (8.15)$$

Correspondingly, define the Metropolis–Hastings kernel as:

$$P_{\text{MH}}(x, dy) = q(x, y)\alpha(x, y)dy$$
$$+ \underbrace{\left[1 - \int q(x, y)\alpha(x, y)dy\right]}_{r(x)} \mathbb{1}(x \in dy). \qquad (8.16)$$

For a given value x, the Markov chain moves to $y \neq x$ with probability $q(x, y)\alpha(x, y)$, and stays at $y = x$ with probability $[1 - \int q(x, y)\alpha(x, y)dy] = r(x)$.

- Note that this kernel achieves π as the invariant distribution. As above:

$$\int P_{\text{MH}}(x, A)\pi(x)dx$$

$$= \int \int_A q(x, y)\alpha(x, y)dy\pi(x)dx + \int_A r(x)\pi(x)dx$$

$$= \int_A \int q(x, y)\alpha(x, y)\pi(x)dxdy + \int_A r(x)\pi(x)dx$$

$$= \int_A \int q(y, x)\alpha(y, x)\pi(y)dxdy + \int_A r(x)\pi(x)dx$$

$$= \int_A \left[\int q(y, x)\alpha(y, x)dx\right]\pi(y)dy + \int_A r(x)\pi(x)dx$$

$$= \int_A [1 - r(y)]\pi(y)dy + \int_A r(x)\pi(x)dx$$

$$= \int_A \pi(y)dy = \Pi(A).$$

- This MH kernel can be implemented via simulation: start with x^0, then

— Draw "candidate" y_1 from the conditional density $q(x^0, y_1)$.

— Set $x^1 = \begin{cases} y_1 \text{ with probability } \alpha(x^0, y_1) \\ x^0 \text{ with probability } 1 - \alpha(x^0, y_1). \end{cases}$

— Now draw candidate y_2 from the conditional density $q(x^1, y_2)$.

— Set $x^2 = \begin{cases} y_2 \text{ with probability } \alpha(x^1, y_2) \\ x^1 \text{ with probability } 1 - \alpha(x^1, y_2). \end{cases}$

— And so on.

According to the Markov chain theory, for N large enough, we have approximately:

$$\Pi(A) \approx \frac{1}{N} \sum_{i=\tau>1}^{\tau+N} \mathbb{1}(x^i \in A).$$

Here τ refers to the length of an initial "burn-in" period, when the Markov chain is still converging.

• What are choices for the conditional density $q(\theta, \theta')$? Two common options are:

— Random walk: $q(x, y) = q_1(y - x)$, where q_1 is a density function, e.g., $N(0, \sigma^2)$. According to this approach, the candidate $y = x + \epsilon$, $\epsilon \sim N(0, \sigma^2)$, and so it is called a random walk density.

— Independent draws: $q(x, y) = q_2(y)$, where q_2 is a density function. The candidate y is independent of x (However, because the candidate is sometimes rejected, with probability $1 - \alpha(x, y)$, the resulting random sequence still exhibits dependence).

— Gibb's sampler: Consider the case when x and y are both multidimensional, i.e., $x = (x_1, x_2)$; $y = (y_1, y_2)$, and consider some joint density $g(x)$ for x and y, with associated conditionals $g(x_1|x_2)$ and $g(x_2|x_1)$. Then set

$$q(x, y) = g(y_2|y_1) \cdot g(y_1|x_2).$$

That is, for a given $x = (x_1, x_2)$, first you draw y_1 according to the conditional density $g(y_1|x_2)$, then you draw y_2 according to the conditional density $g(y_2|y_1)$.

8.2.3 Application to Bayesian posterior inference

- For Bayesian inference, the desired density is the posterior density $f(\theta|\vec{z})$ (where $\vec{z}$ denotes the data information). We want to construct a Markov chain, using the MH idea, such that its invariant distribution is the posterior distribution of $\theta|\vec{z}$.
- We use θ and θ' to denote the "current" and "next" draws of θ from the Markov chain.
- Recall that $f(\theta|\vec{z}) \propto f(\vec{z}|\theta)f(\theta)$, the likelihood function times the prior density. Hence, the MH fudge factor is

$$\alpha(\theta,\theta') = \min\left[\frac{\pi(\theta')q(\theta',\theta)}{\pi(\theta)q(\theta,\theta')},1\right]$$

$$= \min\left[\frac{f(\vec{z}|\theta')f(\theta')q(\theta',\theta)}{f(\vec{z}|\theta)f(\theta)q(\theta,\theta')},1\right].$$

So you are more likely to accept a draw θ' relative to θ if the likelihood ratio is higher.

- For a given $q(x,y)$, drawing a sequence $\theta^1,\theta^2,\ldots,\theta^n,\ldots$ such that, for n large enough, each θ^n can be treated as a draw with marginal distribution equal to $\pi(\theta|\vec{z})$. Hence, for instance, the posterior mean can be approximated as:

$$\mathbb{E}[\theta|\vec{z}] \approx \frac{1}{N}\sum_{i=\tau}^{\tau+N}\theta^i.$$

- In the multidimensional case when $\theta = (\theta_1,\theta_2)$, when $q(\theta,\theta')$ is the Gibb's sampler, then you could take the joint density of θ to be the desired posterior density $f(\theta|\vec{z})$ itself, and take the Gibb's sampler to be

$$q(\theta,\theta') = f(\theta'_2|\theta'_1;\vec{z})\cdot f(\theta'_1|\theta_2;\vec{z}).$$

This is useful when the full posterior $f(\theta|\vec{z})$ is difficult to sample from directly, but the individual conditionals are easy to characterize and sample from.

Moreover, when data augmentation is performed, you could also use Gibb's sampling, and interpret θ_1 as the parameters of the model, while θ_2 are the latent variables.

Bibliography

Chib, S., and E. Greenberg (1995): "Understanding the Metropolis-Hastings Algorithm," *Am. Stat.*, **49**, 327–335.

Gourieroux, C., and A. Monfort (1996): *Simulation-Based Econometric Methods*. Oxford University Press.

Hajivassiliou, V., and P. Ruud (1994): "Classical Estimation Methods for LDV Models Using Simulation," in *Handbook of Econometrics*, Vol. 4, eds. by R. Engle and D. McFadden. North Holland.

McFadden, D. (1989): "A Method of Simulated Moments for Estimation of Discrete Response Models without Numerical Integration," *Econometrica*, **57**, 995–1026.

Chapter 9

Problem Sets

Problem Set: Numerical Integration and Simulation

In this problem set, we will explore numerical integration and simulation. For simulation, we will illustrate importance sampling, and also the GHK recursive approach.

1. Consider computing the mean of a univariate standard normal distribution, truncated to the region [0,1]:

$$E(x) = \frac{\int_0^1 x\phi(x)dx}{\int_0^1 \phi(x)dx},$$

where $\phi(x)$ denotes the standard normal density.

(1a) Compute $E(x)$ explicitly, using quadrature routines (e.g., quad in Matlab). Use this as the "true value" of $E(x)$.

(1b) Simulate using a "crude" accept–reject routine:

Take 50 random draws x^s from $N(0,1)$. Reject the draws which lie outside the truncation region. Take average of the nonrejected draws,

$$\frac{\sum_s x^s * \mathbf{1}(x^s \in [0,1])}{\sum_s \mathbf{1}(x^s \in [0,1])},$$

as an estimate of $E(x)$.

Repeat this 100 times to get 100 estimates of $E(x)$. Characterize the distribution of these estimates (i.e., mean, median, standard deviation, etc.).

(1c) Simulate using importance sampling:

Take 50 random draws x^s from $U[0,1]$. Multiply each draw by the importance sampling weight, which in this case is just $w^s = \dfrac{\phi(x^s)}{\int_0^1 \phi(s)ds}$. Take average of the weighted draws,

$$\frac{1}{50} \sum_s x^s w^s,$$

as an estimate of $E(x)$.

Repeat this 100 times to get 100 estimates of $E(x)$. Characterize the distribution of these estimates (i.e., mean, median, standard deviation, etc.).

Compare the accuracy of the results in (1b) and (1c).

2. Now we consider a bivariate example. Let (x,y) be distributed according to the bivariate normal density $BN(0,0,1,1,0.5)$, the bivariate density with zero mean $[0,0]'$ and variance matrix $\Sigma = \begin{bmatrix} 1 & \frac{1}{2} \\ \frac{1}{2} & 1 \end{bmatrix}$, but truncated to the region $x \in [0,1]$; $y \in [-1,2]$.
   Consider calculating

$$E(xy) = \frac{\int_0^1 \int_{-1}^2 xy\phi(x,y)dydx}{\int_0^1 \int_{-1}^2 \phi(x,y)dydx},$$

where $\phi(x,y)$ denotes the density of the bivariate normal distribution described above.

(2a) Compute $E(xy)$ explicitly, using quadrature routines. This requires double integration routines, such as `dblquad` in Matlab. Use this as the "true value" of $E(xy)$.

(2b) Simulate using a "crude" accept–reject routine:

Take 100 random draws x^s, y^s from $\phi(x,y)$. As we described in class, one way to do this is to draw

u^s, v^s, independently from the $N(0,1)$ distribution, then transform them to the desired draws as

$$\begin{pmatrix} x^s \\ y^s \end{pmatrix} = \Sigma^{1/2} \cdot \begin{pmatrix} u^s \\ v^s \end{pmatrix},$$

where $\Sigma^{1/2}$ denotes the lower-triangular Cholesky factorization of Σ (make sure that you use the lower triangular version).

Then reject the draws which lie outside the truncation region. Take average of the nonrejected draws

$$\frac{\sum_s x^s \cdot y^s \cdot \mathbf{1}(x^s \in [0,1], y^s \in [-1,2])}{\sum_s \mathbf{1}(x^s \in [0,1], y^s \in [-1,2])},$$

as an estimate of $E(xy)$.

Repeat this 100 times to get 100 estimates of $E(xy)$. Characterize the distribution of these estimates (i.e., mean, median, standard deviation, etc.).

(2c) Simulate using GHK:

Generate 100 random draws of (x^s, y^s) using the recursive GHK algorithm. For each draw, also calculate the associated truncation probability τ^s (as defined in lecture notes).

Estimate $E(xy)$ as

$$\frac{\sum_s x^s \cdot y^s \cdot \tau^s}{\sum_s \tau^s}.$$

Repeat this 100 times to get 100 estimates of $E(xy)$. Characterize the distribution of these estimates (i.e., mean, median, standard deviation, etc.).

Compare the accuracy of the results in (2b) and (2c).

Problem Set: BLP Methodology

Attached is a table of market shares, prices, and characteristics on the top-selling brands of cereal in 1992 (Table 9.1). The data

Table 9.1:   Brand Characteristics.

Name	Avg transaction Price ($/lb)	Avg Shelf Price ($/lb)	Avg Ad Expn	In-Sample Market Share	Sgmnt	Cals	Fat	Sugar
1 KGᵃ Corn Flakes	1.81	1.95	7.109[b]	5.67[c]	Fam	100	0	2
2 GM Cheerios	3.16	3.47	7.287	4.38	Fam	110	2	1
3 KG Rice Krispies	2.96	3.20	6.034	4.04	Fam	120	0	3
4 KG Frosted Flakes	2.52	2.68	7.867	3.82	Fam	120	0	13
5 KG Raisin Bran	2.34	2.50	5.591	2.73	Fam	200	1.5	18
6 GM Total	3.61	4.04	3.926	2.36	Adult	110	1	5
7 GM HoneyNut Cheerios	3.14	3.41	4.030	2.26	Fam	120	1.5	11
8 KG Special K	3.48	3.78	3.531	2.16	Adult	110	0	3
9 PT Grape Nuts	2.14	2.29	6.740	2.12	Adult	200	1	7
10 NB SpoonSize ShdWt	2.81	3.05	0.025	2.08	Adult	170	0.5	0
11 QK 100% Natural	2.24	2.55	1.612	1.96	Adult	220	8	13.5
12 KG Frosted Mini Wheats	2.62	2.75	6.106	1.84	Adult	170	1	10
13 KG NutriGrain	2.87	3.10	2.508	1.55	Adult	100	1	0
14 KG Mueslix	3.31	3.58	1.975	1.53	Adult	200	4	13
15 GM Wheaties	2.55	2.86	2.257	1.52	Fam	110	1	4
16 PT Raisin Bran	2.23	2.57	4.361	1.46	Fam	190	1	20
17 RL Muesli	3.34	3.93	0.215	1.26	Adult	210	2.7	14
18 KG Corn Pops	3.51	3.69	3.198	1.46	Fam	120	0	14

19	GM Raisin Nut Bran	2.98	3.22	1.659	1.35	Adult	210	4.5	16
20	GM Basic 4	3.27	3.63	2.510	1.31	Adult	210	3	12
21	GM Cocoa Puffs	3.46	3.67	2.097	1.28	Kids	120	1	14
22	GM Golden Grahams	3.24	3.54	2.953	1.24	Kids	120	1	11
23	GM Cinn. Toast Crunch	3.36	3.56	2.963	1.23	Kids	130	3	10
24	KG Froot Loops	3.53	3.76	3.110	1.20	Kids	120	1	15
25	KG Low Fat Granola	2.68	3.10	2.327	1.17	Adult	190	3	12
26	GM Trix	3.96	4.22	3.236	1.13	Kids	120	1.5	13
27	GM Triples	2.33	2.80	3.036	1.12	Adult	120	1	6
28	KG Crispix	3.28	3.49	3.225	1.12	Adult	110	0	3
29	GM Kix	3.67	3.93	3.801	1.08	Kids	120	0.8	6
30	GM Lucky Charms	3.45	3.72	3.079	1.08	Kids	120	1	13
31	GM AppleCinn. Cheerios	3.02	3.35	3.120	1.06	Fam	120	2	13
32	KG Cracklin Oat Bran	3.19	3.51	2.279	1.06	Adult	190	6	15
33	NB Big Biscuit ShdWt	2.79	3.05	0.000	0.99	Adult	156	1.2	9.6
34	PT Honey Bunches of Oats	2.85	3.18	3.749	0.95	Adult	125	2.2	6
35	PT Great Graines	2.90	3.43	2.648	0.89	Adult	215	5.5	10.5
36	GM Otml Raisin Crisp	2.71	3.04	1.641	0.97	Adult	210	2.5	19

(*Continued*)

Table 9.1: (*Continued*)

Name	Avg transaction Price ($/lb)	Avg Shelf Price ($/lb)	Avg Ad Expn	In-Sample Market Share	Sgmnt	Cals	Fat	Sugar
37 QK Oat Squares	2.43	2.71	1.472	0.94	Adult	220	3	9
38 RL Rice Chex	3.40	3.53	0.875	0.89	Adult	120	0	2
39 GM Total Raisin Bran	3.00	3.50	1.874	0.89	Adult	180	1	19
40 KG Product 19	3.38	3.70	1.408	0.89	Adult	100	0	4
41 KG Apple Jacks	3.64	3.91	1.465	0.84	Kids	120	1	16
42 QK Capt Crunch	2.55	2.86	1.714	0.83	Kids	105	1.5	11.5
43 NB Shredded Wheat	2.82	3.00	2.925	0.80	Adult	160	0.5	0
44 PT Fruity Pebbles	3.21	3.48	1.710	0.83	Kids	110	1	12
45 GM Clusters	3.14	3.52	1.425	0.78	Fam	210	3.5	14
46 KG Cinnamon MiniBuns	2.75	3.14	0.002	0.76	Fam	120	0.5	12
47 KG Double Dip Crunch	3.01	3.52	1.454	0.73	Adult	110	0	11
48 GM MultiGrain Cheerios	3.34	3.74	2.520	0.75	Fam	110	1	15
49 PT Honeycomb	3.40	3.67	2.567	0.74	Kids	110	0	11
50 QK Popeye	1.77	1.77	0.000	0.67	Kids	120	1	13.3
51 basket of all other brands	2.68	1.77	0.645[d]	24.29				

[a]KG: Kelloggs; GM: General Mills; PT: Post (Phillip Morris); RL: Ralston; QK: Quaker Oats.
[b]quarterly expns, $million. *Source: AD$Summary* Avg'd over 1991:ii—1993:ii.
[c]Share of total in-sample purchases. *Source:* Author's calculation from IRI scanner dataset.
[d]Sum of average quarterly advertising expenditure for *all* the nontop 50 brands.

are aggregated from household-level scanner data (collected at supermarket checkout counters).

The market shares below are shares of *total cereal purchases* observed in the dataset. For the purposes of this problem set, assume that all households purchased some cereal during 1992 (so that nonpurchase is not an option).[1] Assume that brand #51, the composite basket of "all other brands," is the outside good.

Two sets of prices are given in the table. *Shelf prices* are those listed on supermarket shelves, and do not include coupon discounts. *Transactions prices* are prices actually paid by consumers, net of coupon discounts. Estimate using the transactions prices. Note that you should subtract the price of brand #51, the "outside good," from the prices of the top 50 brands.

Assume a utility specification for u_{ij}, household i's utility from brand j:

$$u_{ij} = X_j \beta - \alpha p_j + \xi_j + \nu_{ij},$$

where X_j are characteristics of brand j, ξ_j is an unobserved (to the econometrician) quality parameter for brand j, and ν_{ij} is a disturbance term which is identicially and independently distributed (i.i.d.) over households i and brands j. Denote the mean utility level from brand j as

$$\delta_j \equiv X_j \beta - \alpha p_j + \xi_j.$$

1. Assuming that the ν_{ij}'s are distributed i.i.d. type I extreme value, derive the resulting expressions for the market shares of each brand j, $j = 1, \ldots, 51$.

   Next we implement the BLP two-step estimator.

2. Invert the resulting system of demand functions to get estimates of the mean utility levels δ_j as a function of the shares s_j.

---

[1] This is not far from the truth; from an alternative data source (the *IRI Marketing FactBook*), one finds out that in 1992, 97.1% of American households purchased at least some cereal during the year.

3. Estimate the second stage regression of δ_j on X_j and p_j in different ways:

   (a) OLS.
   (b) 2SLS: using average characteristics for all other brands produced by the same manufacturer as brand j as instruments for p_j.
   (c) 2SLS: using average characteristics for all other brands produced by rivals to the manufacturer as brand j as instruments for p_j.
   (d) 2SLS: using average characteristics for all other brands as instruments for p_j.

   How does your results differ?

4. From the aggregate demand functions derived in question 1, derive the formulas for the derivatives $\frac{\partial s_j}{\partial p_{j'}}$ and the elasticities $\epsilon_{ij} \equiv \frac{\partial s_j}{\partial p_{j'}} \frac{p_{j'}}{s_j}$, where j and j' are any two pairs of brands. What is the difference between ϵ_{ik} and ϵ_{jk}. Explain the implication of this.

5. Assuming that the manufacturers of the top 50 brands compete in Bertrand fashion, derive the 50 first-order conditions which define prices in this market, assuming constant marginal costs of production for each brand (and ignoring advertising costs). In other words, assume that the total cost function for brand j $C_j(q_j) = c_j q_j$.

   These FOCs are a system of *linear* equations in the unknowns $c_1, \ldots, c_{50}$. Using the expression derived in question 4 above, rewrite these FOCs completely in terms of the known prices, shares, and parameters (in particular, α).

6. Solve for the marginal costs from this system of equations. Recall that linear equations of the form $Ax = b$ can be solved by $x = A^{-1}b$.

   After deriving these costs, solve for the markup $\frac{p_j - c_j}{p_j}$ associated with each brand.

Problem Set: Single-agent Dynamic Discrete-Choice (DDC) Models

In this problem set, we will explore computation and estimation of single-agent DDC models, with an emphasis on the Harold Zurcher (HZ) model.

1. Compute the HZ model.

   - Use the parameter estimates θ from the top of Table X in Rust's (1987) paper.
   - Compute $\mathrm{EV}(x, i; \theta)$ using the value iteration procedure, described in Rust paper (and lecture notes).
   - Graph $\mathrm{EV}(x, i; \theta)$, separately for $i = 0, 1$.

2. Simulate the HZ model.

   - Assume there are $N = 100$ homogeneous buses, and you observe each for $T = 10{,}000$ weeks. HZ makes replacement decision every week.
   - Initial values: take $x_{n0} = 0$, $i_{n0} = 0$ for all buses n.
   - For each week t, simulate the utility shocks $\epsilon_{0nt}, \epsilon_{1nt}$, the mileage x_{nt}, and replacement decision i_{nt}:

     — Draw $\epsilon_{0nt}, \epsilon_{1nt}$, independently from Type I extreme value distribution, with CDF $F(\epsilon) = \exp[-\exp(-(\epsilon - 0.577))].$[2]
     — Draw mileage x_{nt} from transition $G(x|x_{n,t-1}, i_{n,t-1})$, which is multinomial as given in Rust paper.
     — Compute replacement decision

     $$i_{nt} \equiv \mathrm{argmax}_{i=0,1} \left(u(x_{nt}, i; \theta) + \epsilon_{int} + \beta \cdot EV(x_{nt}, i; \theta) \right),$$

     where you use $EV(x_{nt}, i; \theta)$ as computed in problem #1.

   - After sequences of x, i are simulated for all buses, provide summary statistics of your simulated data.

---

[2]To simulate from a desired CDF $F(x)$, draw uniform random variables $u \sim U[0, 1]$, and transform $x = F^{-1}(u)$.

3. Estimate the model using Rust's MLE/nested-fixed-point algorithm.
4. Estimate the model using the indirect Hotz–Miller method.

Auctions: problems

1. Implement the Guerre, Perrigne, and Vuong (2000) procedure for an IPV auction model:

   - Generate 1,000 valuations $x \sim U[0,1]$. Recall (as derived in lecture notes) the equilibrium bid function in this case is

   $$b(x) = \frac{N-1}{N} \cdot x.$$

   - For 500 of the valuations, split them into 125, 4-bidder auctions. For each of these valuations, calculate the corresponding equilibrium bid.
   - For the other 500 valuations, split them into 100, 5-bidder auctions. For each of these valuations, calculate the corresponding equilibrium bid.
   - For each b_i, compute the estimated valuation $\tilde{x}_i$ using the GPV equation:

   $$\frac{1}{g(b_i)} = (N_i - 1)\frac{x_i - b_i}{G(b_i)}$$

   $$\Leftrightarrow x_i = b_i + \frac{G(b_i)}{(N_i - 1)g(b_i)},$$

   (where N_i denotes the number of bidders in the auction that the bid b_i is from).
   In computing the G and g functions, try,

   1. Epanechnikov kernel ($\mathcal{K}(u) = \frac{3}{4}(1 - u^2)\mathbf{1}(|u| \le 1)$)
   2. Uniform kernel ($\mathcal{K}(u) = \frac{1}{2}\mathbf{1}(|u| \le 1)$).

   Also, try different bandwidths $h \in \{0.5, 0.1, 0.05, 0.01\}$.

   For each case, plot x vs. $\tilde{x}$. Can you comment on performance of the procedure for different bandwidth values?

   - Compute and plot the empirical CDF's for the estimated valuations $\tilde{x}_i$, separately for $N = 4$ and $N = 5$.

2. Consider an example of a common-value model with conditionally independent signals, drawn from Matthew (1984). Namely

⇒ Pareto-distributed common values: $v \sim g(v) = \alpha v^{-(\alpha+1)}$, with support $v \in [1, +\infty)$. Note that corresponding CDF is $G(v) = 1 - v^{-\alpha}$.

⇒ Conditionally independent signals: $x|v \sim U[0, v]$.

⇒ Equilibrium bidding strategy:

$$b(x) = \left[\frac{N - 1 + \max(1, x)^{-N}}{N}\right] \cdot \left(\frac{N + \alpha}{N + \alpha - 1}\right) \cdot \max(1, x).$$
$$(9.1)$$

So do the following:

- Simulate the common values v_t i.i.d. from $G(v)$,[3] for $t = 1, 225$ (225 auctions).
- For each auction $t = 1, 125$, generate 4 signals each, where $x_{it} \sim U[0, v_t]$, for $i = 1, \ldots, 4$, and $t = 1, \ldots, 125$.

  Then for each signal x_{it}, generate the corresponding equilibrium bid b_{it} for a 4-bidder auction, using Eq. (9.1).

  For each bid b_{it}, pick out the maximum among rivals' bids in auction t: $b*_{it} \equiv \max_{j \neq i} b_{jt}$.

  For each bid in the simulated 4-bidder auctions, recover the corresponding pseudovalue $\xi(b_{it}, N_t)$, using Eq. (10) from auction lecture notes.

- For each auction $t = 126, 225$, generate 5 signals each, where $x_{it} \sim U[0, v_t]$, for $i = 1, \ldots, 5$, and $t = 126, \ldots, 225$.

  As above, generate the corresponding b_{it}, $b*_{it}$ for each signal. Then, for each bid in these 5-bidder auctions, recover the pseudovalue $\xi(b_{it}, N_t)$.

- Compute and plot the empirical CDF's for the estimated pseudovalues $\xi(b_{it}, N_t)$, separately for $N_t = 4$ and $N_t = 5$.

---

[3]To simulate from any nonuniform CDF, use the "inverse-quantile" procedure. Generate $w \sim U[0, 1]$, then transform $v = G^{-1}(x)$. The random variable $v \sim G(v)$.

Bibliography

Matthews, S. (1984): "Information Acquisition in Discriminatory Auctions," in *Bayesian Models in Economic Theory*, eds. by M. Boyer and R. Kihlstrom, North-Holland.

Index

Printed in the United States
By Bookmasters